MISHA GLOUBERMAN WITH SHEILA HETI

THE CHAIRS ARE WHERE
THE PEOPLE GO

MISHA GLOUBERMAN is a performer, facilitator, and artist who lives in Toronto.

SHEILA HETI is the author of three books of fiction: *The Middle Stories*, *Ticknor*, and *How Should a Person Be?*. Her writing has appeared in *The New York Times*, *McSweeney's*, *n + 1*, and *The Guardian*. She regularly conducts interviews for *The Believer*.

THE CHAIRS ARE WHERE THE PEOPLE GO

THE CHAIRS ARE WHERE THE PEOPLE GO

How to Live, Work, and Play in the City

MISHA GLOUBERMAN

WITH SHEILA HETI

ff

Faber and Faber, Inc.

An affiliate of Farrar, Straus and Giroux

New York

Faber and Faber, Inc.
An affiliate of Farrar, Straus and Giroux
18 West 18th Street, New York 10011

Distributed in Canada by D&M Publishers, Inc.
Printed in the United States of America
First edition, 2011

An excerpt from *The Chairs Are Where the People Go*
originally appeared in *The Believer*.

Library of Congress Cataloging-in-Publication Data
Glouberman, Misha, [date].
The chairs are where the people go : how to live, work, and play
in the city / Misha Glouberman, with Sheila Heti.
    p.   cm.
ISBN 978-0-86547-945-6 (alk. paper)
1. Group problem solving.   2. Group relations training.
3. Happiness.   4. Group games.   5. Improvisation (Acting).
I. Heti, Sheila, [date].   II. Title.

HD30.29.G585 2011
650.1—dc22

                                           2010047600

Designed by Jonathan D. Lippincott
Frontispiece illustrations by Leanne Shapton

www.fsgbooks.com

1   3   5   7   9   10   8   6   4   2

The names and circumstances of some people have been changed,
and some people are composites.

The authors would like to thank the Ontario Arts Council for the grant they
received to work on the book. The Ontario Arts Council is an agency of
the Government of Ontario.

To Margaux

Contents

Foreword

Misha Glouberman is my very good friend. Years ago, we started a lecture series together called Trampoline Hall, at which amateurs speak on random subjects in a bar. He was the host, and I picked the lecturers and helped them choose their topics. I was interested in finding people who were reticent about talking, rather than showy people who wanted an opportunity to perform. After three years of working on the show, I quit, but Misha kept it running.

A few years later, I really missed working with Misha, so I decided I would write a book about him. It was called *The Moral Development of Misha*. I got about sixty pages into the story of a man who wandered the city, who was nervous about his career and his life, yet was a force of reason in any situation. Work on it stalled, however, when I couldn't figure out how to develop him morally.

Worse than that, I never found the project as interesting as talking to my friend. I have always liked the way Misha speaks and thinks, but writing down the sorts of things he *might* say and think was never as pleasurable as encountering the things he actually *did* say and think. If I wanted to capture Misha, in all his specificity, why was I creating a fictional Misha? If I wanted to engage with Misha, why not leave my room and walk down the street?

One day, I told him I thought the world should have a book of everything he knows.

He agreed to collaborate on this project with me, but only if I promised *not to quit in the middle as I always do with everything*.

We spent a few days coming up with a list of things he cares about, and those topics became the chapters of this book. Over the next several months, we met a few times a week at my apartment, usually at around ten in the morning. We drank coffee and worked our way down the list. Misha sat across from me at my desk. As he talked, I typed.

Misha speaks in fully formed paragraphs, I was surprised to discover, and the words here are pretty much as he said them. Very infrequently, as he spoke, I would ask a question. I chose the chapters I wanted to include and put them in some kind of order.

As you read the book, Misha may come off as this very opinionated person—but in life he's quite the opposite. He's not the sort of person who goes around giving his take on things. At parties, he can often be found explaining to one person what some other person meant. At Trampoline Hall, Misha leads a Q&A after every lecture, and he is really good at revealing the essence of what each person is trying to communicate. He's usually very reserved and cautious in his opinions, always seeing the other person's side.

Sometimes when he and I spend time together, a more opinionated side of Misha comes out. When we were doing this book, often he would say something, then say to me, "Don't put that in," and then I would say, "But that's the best part," and I would.

We had a really nice time.

—Sheila Heti, Toronto

THE CHAIRS ARE WHERE
THE PEOPLE GO

1. People's Protective Bubbles Are Okay

I hear people complain that, for instance, in this city, people don't say hi on the street or make eye contact on the subway. And people try to remedy this problem by doing public art projects that are meant to rouse the bourgeoisie from their slumber. But that's ridiculous! It's perfectly reasonable for people not to want to see your dance performance when they are coming home from work. People are on the subway because they're getting from one place to another, and for all you know, they're coming from a job that involves interacting with lots and lots of people, and going to a home where there's a family where they're going to interact with lots more people. And the subway's the one place where they can have some quiet time, get some reading done, *not* have to smile, *not* have to make eye contact. That's what a city is: a city is a place where you can be alone in public, and where you have that right. It's *necessary* to screen people out. It would be *overwhelming* if you had to perceive every single person on a crowded subway car in the fullness of their humanity. It would be completely paralyzing. You couldn't function. So don't try to fix this. There is no problem.

2. How to Make Friends in a New City

If you're just finishing school—maybe you're in your early twenties, maybe you're moving to a new city—you need to make friends. The very most important thing to know is that this isn't easy. It's really easy to make friends when you're a child, and it's really easy to make friends in high school and in college. And for a lot of people, I think, it's a real shock to discover that making friends doesn't take care of itself in adulthood. When you come to university you're crammed together with a couple of thousand people who are around your age and who share a bunch of stuff in common with you, and most important, are at that very same moment also looking for new friends. In this sort of situation, it would take a lot of conscious effort to end up *not* having friends. But adult life isn't like that. You may move to a new city, maybe for a job that doesn't easily put you into contact with a lot of people with whom you have much in common. So what that means is that it's *work*, and maybe for the first time in your life you have to actually take making friends on as a project. I knew so many people around that stage of life who suddenly found themselves isolated and couldn't understand why, and had never thought of making friends as something they had to bring conscious effort to.

If you see making friends as a project, you can understand that there will be efforts and costs and risks. You have to go to functions that you don't exactly feel like going to, you have to stick your neck out and make gestures that are embarrassing or can make you feel vulnerable. You'll have to spend time with people who initially seem interesting but then turn out not to be.

4

But all those things are okay if you see them as the costs involved in a project.

It's useful to identify what you like to do, because friends are the people with whom you can do those things. So if you like to cook, you might take a cooking class and meet people who are interested in cooking. Or if what you like to do is go drink in bars, then find people who want to drink in bars with you. If you like to watch television and make fun of it, find other people who want to do that. It's useful to remember that friendship needs an activity associated with it.

If you're the ambitious sort, you can try to create your own world around you, and maybe have a party at your house every two weeks. I think Andy Warhol's grandmother gave him similar advice. This gets you more than friends—it can create a whole community. I'll say it takes a certain kind of person to do this, though. But if you *can* do it—if you can put yourself at the center of something—it really works.

When I came to Toronto, here's what I liked to do: I liked drinking in bars and I liked thinking about the Internet. This was at a time when thinking about the Internet wasn't so popular, but drinking in bars was, so I just started a club, and I put out the word, and I invited other people. I was the only person at my organization at the time who was really interested in thinking about the Internet. It was at a time when sort of every organization hired one person to be their web guy. So there were all these lonely, isolated web guys scattered around the city, and we started a biweekly bar night. I was completely new in town, but just by starting something like that, you really put yourself in the center of all kinds of things. Being a host—it's a really super-valuable service that a lot of people are disinclined to do, and if you can do it, it's a great way to meet people.

3. The Uniqlo Game

There's an online game which I love—from, of all places, a Japanese clothing company called Uniqlo. The game has a fast-paced pop culture feel to it. There is a grid of Uniqlo logos on the screen, and you manipulate them in different ways. You can make big ones or little ones. You can chop them up or merge them together. You can make them disappear. It's a multiplayer game. All they tell you about the players is their sign-in name and what country they're from, so you and someone in France and someone in Korea and someone in the United States, all of indeterminate age and gender, are manipulating these shared sets of blocks.

The genius of the game, to me, is that there's no chat area. There's no way you can send messages to the other players. You can only communicate by dragging these logos around. It's so interesting in the context of that to think, *Can I make this person in Korea like me? Can I flatter this person in France by echoing the moves that they're making on this grid? Can I do something terribly mischievous in a way that won't be perceived as hostile, or can I do something hostile in a way that will be?*

I like playing this game a lot.

4. Going to the Gym

One idea that came up a lot around the time I was in college was that some ideas or opinions were social constructions. So, for instance, if you could show that ideals of female beauty were something that *society* had created, then you could also show that these ideals aren't something that people naturally feel, but rather they're a brainwashing tool created by society—in this case to perpetuate the patriarchal hegemony.

Another example of this: I read a book a little while ago which made the point that while we worry a lot about status, maybe we shouldn't, since after all, the things that are associated with status in our society aren't associated with status in other societies right now, and weren't associated with status historically in other societies, so really it's all arbitrary. Today, being thin and having strong analytic skills are valued, whereas in another society being a fast runner would have been important, or in another one, obesity was a sign of status. The author sort of concludes, *Why worry?*

But all that stuff's crazy! Just because something's socially constructed, doesn't mean it's not real. I mean, we can show that every society has a different set of standards for feminine beauty, and that every society has different sets of standards for status, but it's equally remarkable that every society *does* have standards for feminine beauty, and *does* have standards for status. We're humans. We exist in societies. We create cultures. And these cultures may be different from each other, with different beliefs, but they're who we are. There's not something more "real" to discover about us if you take all that away. A human who doesn't exist in a culture isn't somehow more true. In fact, I think a human who doesn't exist in a culture—that's not what a human *is*. I exist in the culture that I exist in, and I can know that other cultures see status in different ways, but I will be swayed by the ideas of status that affect mine. I can know that other cultures have different standards of feminine beauty and still be attracted by the standards of feminine beauty that exist in mine.

This doesn't seem any more shocking to me than finding a passage of literature written in English beautiful but not a passage written in a language I can't read. I don't feel like my impression of beauty in the English passage is destroyed by someone pointing out that the correlation between these words and the objects they describe isn't actually *real*—that other societies use different words for the same things, and that the use of one symbol to represent a certain object or sound is at base somewhat arbitrary. I'm okay with that.

I went to the gym pretty regularly for a long time, and it always felt so crazy to me. The gym is like the meeting point of all these different things that are emblematic of our time. It looks like the shopping mall and the factory, and it's where our crazy desire to exert ourselves and work hard meets our crazy desire to be young forever, along with our crazy confusion about our appetites, and our imagining that we can subject everything to rational, super-mechanistic processes. Fifty years from now, if you wanted to pick something that encapsulates the old days of the early twenty-first century, you'd show the gym.

For a while I was kind of embarrassed to be a part of what seems like a huge fad of our day, but then I figured: Fuck it. I *am* of our day. I don't have to see through everything. Or I can even see through things a little bit, but I'm still a part of them.

5. How to Be Good at Playing Charades

I have taught How to Be Good at Playing Charades in a bunch of contexts. I have taught corporate charades classes. I've taught charades as part of a regular games night I ran at a hotel, and I taught it on the radio. The most fun was teaching charades as a six-part series of classes that people signed up for. They paid me money to come to a classroom every week. We did charades drills and exercises. Sometimes I gave them homework. I gave out charades certificates at the end.

For reasons that are completely unclear to me, I was very nervous about whether I was qualified to teach charades. This is crazy! I'm perfectly okay with teaching a music class to trained musicians, even though I don't read music or really know anything about it, but for some reason I was worried that my qualifications as a charades expert might be challenged.

So I did something I never do in my classes, which was that I really tried to establish my authority on the first day. People acted out clues, and we would collectively try to guess them, and I would guess the clue before everyone else in the class every single time. I felt like some old martial arts instructor, challenging people in the class to try to push him over as a way to win their respect. I did this consciously.

When I planned my first charades class, I worked really hard on the announcement because I didn't think anyone would sign up. I figured that just sending out the announcement might constitute the whole project, but I was pleasantly surprised when quite a lot of people signed up.

A lot of people also dropped out. I think they dropped out when they realized it really *was* just a course in charades. I think they expected there to be something else happening.

There are basically two sets of skills for playing charades. There are acting-related skills and guessing-related skills—sort of like fielding and hitting in baseball, or offense and defense in hockey.

When you're acting out a clue for another person, it's really important to remember that the other person does not know what you're acting out. This seems obvious, but a lot of the time, people will act out a charade in a way which would make perfect sense if you *knew* what the title was, but from which the title would be completely impossible to guess if you didn't know it.

This seems like a trivial point, but it's important. It means that, if at all possible, you shouldn't get angry at the other person for not knowing what it is you're trying to act out. It's one of the most common failures that people have: they'll act something out, and the other person won't be able to guess it, and their response will be to do the same gesture again, but more exasperated this time. So the first step really is just an acceptance of the fact that the other person does *not* know.

Some of the tips that apply to charades are the same tips you would apply to any improvisation: Be precise in your gestures. Be wholehearted. Don't forget to bring emotional content to what you do. These things help a lot.

When you're guessing, assume that every detail is important. If someone is drinking a beverage, you might say *drink* or *water*. But if they're drinking a beverage in a dainty manner with their pinkie extended, assume that's part of the clue—that there is a reason for that. The word that they're trying to connote cannot be *drink*, because no one would try to connote the word *drink* by drinking in this very specific manner. The word might be *tea* or *English*.

The most important thing to remember for everyone involved is that it's a dialogue. That is, it's your job to respond to each other. So, as the guesser, throw lots of guesses at the person acting out the clue, because this allows them to change what they are doing, or lets you know if you're on the right or wrong track. If you just sit and watch, waiting until you know for sure, you'll never get it right. Similarly, as the person acting out the clue, if you just take the approach that you want to take, while ignoring what is or isn't getting through to the people you're acting for, it's going to take a very long time.

Playing charades is specifically about the difficulty of communication. Without the difficulty, there is no game. With practice you could get better at communicating through the obstacles that charades presents you, but that's not really the point. It's a game, so the point is not the elimination of obstacles—it's enjoying yourself. To learn to play charades, you have to learn to enjoy yourself while trying to communicate with people who don't understand you and don't know what you know.

6. Don't Pretend There Is No Leader

People are very uncomfortable with roles. They like to pretend they're *not* in charge when they *are* in charge. They like to pretend someone else who *is* in charge is *not* in charge. They don't understand that it can be great to be in charge and it can be great to have someone else in charge—that there can be pleasure in these different roles.

I think a thing that happens a lot in certain kinds of creative groups and certain kinds of activist groups is a pretense that everything is collaborative and nonhierarchical, when in truth someone is the leader. Often that person is the person who started the group.

There are several reasons people pretend they're not the leader. One reason is a simple mistake. The mistake is that they think it's mean to tell people what to do, and they want to be nice. They think that being bossy isn't nice, or having power over people isn't nice. But that's silly! Of course it's oppressive to be someone's leader if you give them no choice—if you force them to have you as a leader—but a lot of the time people *want* someone to be their leader, especially if they've joined your group.

So in exactly the same way that the rules of a game aren't oppressive but let you play the game and are where the fun of the game lies, leadership can be useful. It's what lets you do things. And it's not cruel.

In some cases, people who feel nervous about leading might be taking their leadership too seriously—thinking it's so powerful they have to temper it. Or they might just be scared. It's scary to be in charge, and it's nice to imagine that decisions are someone else's responsibility. Also, they may not realize that people who aren't leaders typically don't *want* to make all the decisions. They don't want to impose their vision. What they specifically appreciate about the leader is that the leader can provide a vision and make decisions. If you started the group, it can be hard to imagine that someone might want to be in your group and *not* be in charge of it, because it's so exciting for you to be in charge of it. That creates a situation where leaders are often disappointed with people in their group, because the leader gives over some power, and the people in the group don't take as much initiative as the leader imagined they would. So the leader is trying to give them something that they think the people in the group desperately and jealously want, but which they actually don't want at all.

I think this happens with bands all the time, and in social justice activism. In these realms, it can be hard because there's often an ideological opposition to the idea of leadership.

So here's the sort of thing that I think happens all the time, and I saw it recently in Toronto. This guy started a band. And he pretty much took most of the responsibility and wrote all the songs and stuff. Then he invited a bunch of friends to join the band, who were really in no way there as equal partners, but nobody acknowledged this. In fact, the official policy was that the band was a collaboration between everyone. Which was a lie—a lie that I think was evident to anybody looking at the situation, but a lie that everyone in the situation had a stake in perpetuating.

What happened eventually is that the consequences of that lie—it's not even a lie, it's willful self-deception—began to make themselves known. The band went on tour and some people got to go and some people didn't, and the people who didn't get to go became angry. Then the band started to make money and the person who started the band wanted to take more of the money than everyone else, and the others got upset. None of that would have happened if people actually knew what their roles were, if they acknowledged them. They would still have had fights, but the fights would have been a lot easier to resolve if the roles had been honest and clear.

It's important to understand that even though someone might be in charge, there's still room for objection. This person can be a complete dictator and there's still room for objection. But at least you know who to direct your objection to. So the person who started the band can say, *We're going to do it this way.* And if you think it's a terrible idea and you know he's in charge, you can express that. Maybe it'll change his mind, maybe it won't, but at least you'll understand what's happening. Otherwise, decisions get made that you don't like and you don't even understand why it is, or you don't understand why this person—who is an equal collaborator and not the leader—is being so bossy. And that's no good. It doesn't work. And it is all born out of a bad politeness.

It's true in a lot of things that if you don't say the difficult thing early, it really fucks you up later on. You might think it hurts people to say to them, early on, *This is my band and I'm in charge,* or *My creative input in this band matters more than yours does,* but saying it early hurts a lot less than dealing with the consequences of not saying it at all.

In many situations there *is* a leader. And that's great. It's a real service to have a leader, most of the time. Leaders do things that other people don't want to do, and which leaders *do* want to do. They make the decisions. They're accountable for those decisions. They take the blame when things go wrong. They do a lot more of the work. And, in creative things, they often do things you're not able to do.

They write good songs for the band, for example.

7. The Chairs Are Where the People Go

There's a thoughtlessness in how people consider their audience that's reflected in how they set up chairs. You can see that thoughtlessness immediately.

An example: There's a literary reading in a large room, and they have a few tables spaced out far from each other near the stage with chairs arranged around them. Behind that they have a couple of rows of chairs, theater-style, then behind *that* there's space for people to stand. Now, this is terrible, and what it reflects is the degree to which the organizers haven't thought about their audience.

Leaving space for people to stand in the back at a reading is ridiculous. Who wants to *stand* through a reading? You're pretty much intentionally designing things so that a lot of people will find the reading boring, because it's incredibly hard not to be bored when you're watching someone read from far away and you're standing. Those people at the back will talk to each other. So not only will they have a bad time, but their bad time will make it worse for everyone else.

By putting those tables and chairs spaced out in front of the stage, you've wasted all this space up front, so you've ensured that the vast majority of the people at the show will be far from the performance. Why do you want that? Everything is better when you're closer to the stage! I've put together a lot of shows, and if you talk to people after, you can always draw a pretty direct correlation between how much people liked the show and how close they sat to the stage.

You have to think about where you put your chairs. For some

events, it's good to have few, if any, chairs. At a cocktail party, you want people to mingle, and if you put down a lot of chairs, people won't move around at all. For a music show or something that people can talk through, the same thing applies. Standing during music is fun because you can dance or talk or move around.

For a play, it's okay to put people fairly close together on raked seating so they can see the stage. It's okay to have them in the dark because they don't need to see each other and the performers don't need to see them.

For a show where the audience's interaction with the performers or with each other is important, it has to be different. As always, you want as many people as possible as close to the stage as possible. You can pack people in tighter than you might think, and they won't mind. If people are drinking, you can scatter a few tables around where they can put their drinks, but you don't need as many as you might think, because every table takes up space where someone might be sitting. You also want to make sure that there's some light on the audience, and if you can, it's great to set things up so the audience can see each other a bit. If you can get them into a quarter-circle around an area that extends from the stage, then the people in the audience can see that they're not alone watching the show.

At a conference, if you want to create a discussion group, you can set up chairs in a circle, and you don't need a table.

If you're going to brunch with a big group of friends, it's better to sit in a circle or something like a circle than to sit at a long table, because then everyone can talk to each other. I hate when you have to sit at a long table, because it means you have to talk to the same five people throughout the whole meal.

Setting up chairs takes a lot of time, but anyone can do it. If you're running a project and you want to get people involved, ask them to set up chairs. People like to set up chairs, and it's easy work to delegate. It's even easier to get people to put chairs away.

Everyone should know these things.

8. How to Teach Charades

When I taught the charades class, I didn't let people play a real game of charades until our second or third meeting, on the assumption that it was important to learn the component skills first, and that it would be irresponsible to cast people into the game without training or warm-ups. Instead we did drills and exercises. Here is a selection:

QUICK SINGLE WORDS IN PAIRS

Before this exercise, give out a million slips of paper to everyone in the class and have them write down individual words. This is a really good thing to have people do before class, while you wait for the stragglers to show up. Then put all of those clues in a bag. Now put the people in pairs and have them take turns acting out these one-word clues for each other. You can tell them that if they find a word too hard, they can skip it and do another one. Have the group do this for three or four minutes. Then have them switch partners and play some more, then switch partners and play some more.

If you do this drill at the beginning of a series, it has a lot of good functions. Everybody gets to play with a lot of other people, so you create a lot of one-to-one camaraderie pretty quickly. And playing in pairs, there's a lot less pressure. Shy people who might otherwise hang back are forced to play.

I'm not sure if I should say this, but the premise that doing one-word clues is easier is false. It's actually harder, because if you have a whole title, you can pick the easy words and do those first, and people will eventually guess the other words if the title is familiar.

Still, I think it's fair. A drill can, in some ways, be harder than a game, in the same way that you might lift weights to prepare to play a sport.

ACTING PRACTICE

Charades is divided into acting skills and guessing skills. Among the acting skills, there's the ability to come up with ideas for gestures, and then there's the ability to communicate those ideas with your body, which is partly about comfort. One thing you can do to train people in comfort is to have the whole group, at once, act out a bunch of words. Take that bag of single words—and it's probably best in this exercise for the class to *be* the thing, rather than *indicate* the thing—and say, *Everybody be a telephone*. This could help people.

CHARADES INSTRUCTION CIRCLE

This drill is played with regular charades clues, not one-word clues. All the participants stand in a circle. One participant takes a clue from the bag and acts it out for the person to their right, who guesses. They're given only thirty seconds to try to complete it. If they fail, the clue gets passed on. Everyone watches.

What's nice about the charades circle is that after each charade is completed, we take a bit of time in the group to talk about what worked and what didn't, and how each person's strategy went.

SPEED DRILLS

Speed is obviously a really important part of charades, so we do speed drills in class. I think that practicing doing charades fast can help get you out of your head, so rather than sort of sitting around trying to think about the best way to go about something, the speed game forces you to go ahead and do it. I think people are more likely to find themselves doing something surprising with their body in a speed game, rather than in a regular game.

You put people in pairs and give them full clues, and give them two minutes during which one person is exclusively the actor and the other person is exclusively the guesser. Tell them their goal is to get as many successful clues as they can during those two minutes, and allow them up to, say, three passes. After each round, have them report back how many clues they were able to guess. This introduces a feeling of competition. Maybe in the first round there are a couple of people who can do five clues in two minutes. Challenge the group to see if anybody can do seven clues in two minutes.

9. Miscommunication Is Nice

I'm very interested in miscommunication. I may have an idea, or a set of ideas, about what an exercise in one of my classes is about, and usually I won't tell the people in class—not because I'm trying to be cryptic, but because my hope is that the exercise is rich enough and complicated enough that they might get something different from it than what I intended.

I think that's what art is: art is communication made in the hope that interesting miscommunications will arise. I tend not to like art when its intention is straightforward, unambiguous communication between the artist and the audience, as in Hollywood movies, for instance, where there's a *message*, or in a lot of political art. Some of those messages I think would be better served through other means. If you have a clear point you want to make, I think a nonfiction book or an editorial might be the best way to make it. If your goal is to literally educate people, there might be better mechanisms than art for doing that.

I'm interested in a mix of communication and miscommunication within a lot of the games, too, like in the gibberish game. When people get practiced at it, communication and miscommunication become richer and more interesting. So rather than hoping the other person will translate your gibberish perfectly, or being surprised that the other person translated it into something other than what you'd intended, there's a third state, which is to feel that the other person said exactly what you intended, but that you didn't know it until you heard it.

10. The Gibberish Game

I think this game comes from Keith Johnstone, who's the inventor of improv as I learned it. I like to play it in my theater classes. The game involves actors speaking in gibberish while other people translate their words for them. This game does a bunch of really wonderful things. Mainly, it makes it impossible for anybody to really be in control.

The general notes I give to the actors who are speaking gibberish is that when you're speaking gibberish, you should use really clear and specific gestures, and as much as possible really enunciate the nonsense words you're saying. Some people like to employ a fancy kind of gibberish language, but I don't care about craft, so I don't care if people say *blah blah blah* if that's what they're comfortable with. It's up to them.

Gibberish makes actors use expression and physicality and tone of voice—basically everything except language—to get things across. There's one kind of gibberish acting in which the actors onstage are such masters of expression and mime that even though they're not using language they all understand exactly what's going on, and the audience understands what's going on, too. I'm not interested in this. What I'm much more interested in is the excitement in the disjunction between actor and translator.

Here's how the game works: There are two actors onstage, and each actor has a translator. An actor says a line of dialogue, and says it with as much specificity and intention as she possibly can. Then as soon as she's spoken, her offstage translator provides an English translation. The translator must translate instinctively.

He has to know what the gibberish means and translate it confidently. Then the second actor speaks and *her* translator translates, and the scene continues this way.

When the game goes well, the idea *isn't* that the translator uncannily gets exactly what the actor was thinking. Rather, with every single translation, the actor is thrown off-balance. She'll say words, thinking she's saying one thing, and then discover that she's actually said something that in some ways is quite similar but in some ways quite different. This happens throughout the scene, and the effect of doing it is giddy and dizzying.

It should feel really natural for everyone involved, which takes just a bit of practice. When the scene is over, people are invariably mistaken about who said what. So an actor will think that she introduced something new into a scene, when really it came from something the translator said that wasn't necessarily present in her sounds or gestures.

One specific note for the translators is to really try to make the text in translation sound as much like the text in gibberish. A cheap joke to make is if someone speaks a really long sentence, to translate it as simply *Yes*. Or, if someone uses a loving tone, to translate it as something really angry. Or if someone acts like a child, to speak as if they're an adult. All those cheap jokes basically constitute refusing to play the game, and the better thing to do is to try and follow the intonations and sounds and rhythms that the actor is speaking, so everyone playing the game is thinking and free-associating at the same time.

There's a fantastic division of labor that occurs, which is wonderful. Every single line of dialogue essentially becomes a collaboration between two people. And everyone's put in a situation where they're not in control.

11. The Residents' Association

My girlfriend, Margaux, and I moved in together a few years ago—or rather, I moved into the apartment next door to hers and we share the two apartments. Just around the time Margaux and I moved in, our neighborhood was changing from a strip of mostly art galleries and refrigerator stores into a neighborhood of trendy martini bars.

A place opened right next door to us that had announced that it was going to be a restaurant but quickly turned out to be a place with a pretty light dinner business and a really active bar business. They played loud music until two-thirty in the morning most nights, often with their doors propped open onto the residential street they faced.

Maybe it's worth saying a bit about how Toronto is laid out. The way the city is arranged, there are a lot of long main streets that go on forever and have, like, three- or four-story residential buildings with storefronts on the ground floor. And then off those streets it's usually purely residential for a few blocks until the next main street.

When I first moved to Toronto I sort of hated this arrangement, because if you want to walk along commercial streets, you can only walk east–west, except very rarely. If you want to get from one commercial street to another, for the most part it's possible only by walking through long residential stretches.

So the bar was on the corner of Queen Street, which is one of those long east–west commercial streets, and Beaconsfield, which is purely residential.

I tried to talk to the owners and manager of the bar to get

them to turn the music down, but it wasn't really effective. They were reasonably nice and sort of sympathetic to my problem, but they weren't great at taking actual steps to turn the music down. I had just moved into this new place, and it was my first time living with a girlfriend, so the stakes seemed maybe even a little higher than they might have otherwise, and it felt like they were making this place very hard for me to live in.

So I started trying to find out what I could do, to see if there were any regulations in the city about noise or how late bars could play loud music and these kinds of things. I did research online and I called a bunch of offices at the City. It was kind of amazing how impossible it was to get information. Then I'd call people at the City who wouldn't return my calls. I'd go through pages and pages on the website which didn't tell me what I needed to know. I'd get conflicting information from different sources. It was really discouraging, partly because I'd always assumed that the system ran a bit better than it does. And the thing I always thought, through this whole process, was that I'm about as resourceful and well positioned as a person could be to get help and information from the system. What would it be like for someone who is not good at online research, or at reading complicated language, or who didn't have as much time to devote as I did?

In the midst of all this, one of the staff at the bar said that the problems were only going to get worse and that I might as well move out. He didn't say this in a mean way. This was genuine advice, born out of sympathy. He even said that *he'd* had to move out of a place in another neighborhood because the music was too loud, and that's the way things go. He said that more bars were going to open in my area, and he told me that the bar next door to me had applied for a license for a 120-person outdoor patio facing onto the residential street that would be open till two in the morning.

That was shocking news. I talked to my city councillor about it, because the licensing decision is basically up to him. He takes his position to council and they go along with it almost all of the time. It turned out that the patio had already been licensed by the provincial liquor board, despite objections by a few vigilant neighbors.

The way the application process works is this: when a place applies for a liquor license, there's a sign posted in the window, which most people don't notice, in which the public are invited to give their opinions for whether the license should be issued. Of course, if people are very vigilant they might notice the sign and get in touch with the licensing board. One of the conditions of the complaints process is that you have to provide your name and your contact information, and agree that this information will be given to the owners of the establishment. But it's almost impossible for you to find out who the owners of the establishment are, what the establishment is, or what the owners' plans for it are. It seems pretty crazy to me that you can't have your complaints be considered privately. If your concern, for instance, is that the people opening the bar next door to your house are the Hell's Angels, you can't complain to the licensing board without the Hell's Angels knowing it was you who complained.

The most important thing, though, is that for all the process and rigmarole, licenses are always issued; while they have a process for public input on the issuing of licenses, as far as I know, licenses are never denied based on the public-input process. Which is just awful.

So at this point I started feeling kind of under siege. I was living in an apartment where every night we heard loud music and yelling and screaming from the bar next door, which doesn't bother some people—it didn't bother Margaux as much—but it bothered me a lot. And then there was the knowledge that the problem would only become worse when the patio opened. The bar owners, in their limited attempts at sympathy, encouraged me to phone when the music was too loud. The music was too loud every night, so every night I would phone, and often they wouldn't answer because the music in the bar was too loud. And

I'd call again, and eventually I would get through. And I would politely ask them to turn the music down, and they would very politely say they would. Then they wouldn't, or they would turn it down but then fifteen minutes later it would become just as loud. This went on night after night and it was infuriating.

One night, when the music was especially loud, I called and I asked the guy to turn the music down, and he apologized and said he would, and a few minutes later the music was even louder, and I was so angry that I went downstairs to talk to him. I opened the door and went inside, and the music was so loud, it was like a punch in the stomach. It was such a terrible feeling to be so upset and wound up and to walk into this place directly underneath your bedroom, jam-packed with sweaty, drunken, well-dressed people from fancier neighborhoods, with music so loud it hurts. And I went up to the bar to get the bartender's attention, and I had to scream to be heard, which makes your adrenaline rush even faster, and I was yelling at him, explaining to him that I was the guy who called from upstairs, and could he please, please, *please* turn the music down. He said, *I'm really busy with a lot of customers, you're going to have to wait about ten minutes*. I had been calling every night for about three months, so I went over to the mixing board, and I figured I'd just turn the music down myself. I've worked mixing boards before. It had little potentiometer knobs instead of sliders, and I went to turn the knob, and my intention was to turn the music down a bit and go upstairs, and I turned the knob, and the music instantly fell silent, and everyone in the room stopped and looked at me. So I was standing there, shaking with anger, in this completely quiet room. The bartender was furious, understandably, and he said something along the lines of, *Don't you ever fucking dare touch that mixer ever again.*

I think it's probably the closest I've come in my adult life both to punching someone and to being punched. And I think it's to the credit of the customers that this didn't happen. Sort of interestingly, the people in the bar seemed to understand what was going on, and a number of people stepped in to diffuse the situation and prevent a fight. They expressed sympathy for my situation, they did all the things that guys in bars do when they tell people to calm down in order to stop fights from happening. And I apologized, because I hadn't meant to turn off the music. The bartender was angry. And I went back upstairs. Then things went back to the way they were before, with me calling down every night, and things being really loud.

It's crazy. Just recalling this story brings back a physiological response. I feel all that stuff happening to me again. And I feel a certain shame. I mean, Margaux didn't mind the noise so much. Part of what was so maddening was the fact that I was the only one being driven nuts. There was a part of me that thought, *I should just ignore this*. It doesn't feel good to be the guy telling people having a good time to stop the party. The fact that it didn't bother Margaux in some ways made the situation a lot more complicated, too, for both of us. Here we were, trying to figure out how to live together, and she has to live with me freaking out every night over something that, to her, isn't really a big deal. And I have to live with her lack of support in dealing with what to me feels like a pressing household problem. So it was hard.

I lived in fear of the patio.

Then I found out that in order for the patio to open, they needed a bunch of things. They needed a liquor license from the province, which they already had. Also, they needed a number of exemptions from zoning laws, which would allow them to construct that patio there, which they'd already been granted, despite the objection of neighbors through a now-familiar public-input process. Finally, they needed a special patio license from the City that allowed them to operate what in the City's terminology is a "boulevard café with a residential flankage." And to do this, it turned out, they needed to get a winning result at a poll of neighbors conducted by the City.

So I talked to the city councillor's office about this, and to the Municipal Licensing and Standards—MLS—office, who are in charge of the poll, and started getting ready to see what I could do to make sure that the neighbors understood what was being voted on, because I'd learned by this point how hard it is to understand the process. I wanted to make sure the neighbors didn't just decide this was another piece of incomprehensible correspondence from the City and something that didn't affect them.

I tried to find out exactly what the timing was for the poll, but that was hard to do. I tried to contact our councillor and the MLS every couple of weeks to find out if they knew when the poll was going to happen, but they never knew exactly. Finally I got in touch with them and asked them *again* when the poll was going to take place, and they told me that it had already happened. The plans for the patio had been approved by a narrow margin. Something like seven people had voted in favor and five people against.

Now, I am a tremendously concerned and engaged citizen in this story. I am someone who has thought of practically nothing but this poll for weeks, and somehow this poll, designed to solicit public input, happened without my knowing it. I asked why, and they told me that only neighbors who own homes are entitled to vote, which was completely infuriating, and which also proved, after several weeks of research, to be false. Then they told me that I was outside the boundaries of the polling area, which turned out, perhaps even more shockingly, to be true. Again: I'm the *next-door neighbor* of this bar. But the regulation says that the vote is held by people who live within five hundred meters of the patio, on the street onto which it will face. The patio was on the corner, which means half the people affected by it had no say.

As I tell this story—when I look back on this time in my life—I find myself a little baffled as to why I was so drawn into this. I put *so much* time into this. But in retrospect, I have sympathy with my past self, when I think about all the details, and about how difficult the situation was; how crazy all the lies and misinformation and obstacles were.

When I heard that the patio had been approved, I went nuts. I think that was the moment that the Queen-Beaconsfield Residents' Association was formed. It seemed so unfair. I was outraged by the sham mechanisms for citizen input. And I was worried that I was going to be driven out of my new apartment and my new domestic arrangement with my girlfriend.

One of the things that the councillor's office had impressed upon me, and which seems entirely fair, is that in any public matter, the concerns of a large number of people are given more weight than the concerns of one person, so as a general rule, if you're having trouble with a noisy bar nearby, one of your first steps should be to find out if other people are having trouble with it, too.

So I started talking to neighbors and finding people who were concerned about this and asking them if they knew other people who were concerned about it and asking them in turn if they knew other people. At first, we had five people, and then ten people, and then twenty people, and then maybe forty people who were all concerned about this bar and how loud it was. Most of these people were completely surprised to learn that the bar was going to open a patio, despite the fact that there had been a public-input process, twice at the municipal level and once at the provincial level.

Of course, it's important to note that once these licenses are granted, they're practically impossible to revoke. So the City gets people's input before any problem arises, then once a problem does arise, the City can go back to those people and say, *Well, you were the ones who voted in favor of it; we asked you for your input—it passed in a popular vote—you should have said something earlier.*

So we formed the Residents' Association, and it was interesting. Most of the time, we don't know much about the neighborhood we live in. The neighborhood that I live in has, within two blocks, about six distinct micro-neighborhoods, and you only see what's relevant to you. So, for instance, one thing that came up later was that the people who went to bars or restaurants in the neighborhood were actually surprised to hear that there was *any* residential use in the neighborhood. They'd say, *No one lives on Queen Street.* But if you look at those buildings, what most of them have is a bar or storefront on the ground floor and what are clearly apartments on the second and third floor. But if you're not looking for those apartments, you don't see them.

In my neighborhood, there are artists and young people living cheaply who rent apartments over the storefronts on Queen, and there are well-off Portuguese families who live in well-kept houses on the north half of the Beaconsfield block, and then there are creative professionals and young, well-off couples in nicer places on the lower half of the Beaconsfield block, and then there's a big apartment building on the corner of my own street that no one notices, that's filled with Vietnamese families living in tiny apartments. All these distinct neighborhoods exist on a single city block, and each of them, I think, is pretty unaware of the others.

So we had meetings and more meetings. People tried to figure out how they could have been understood to have voted in favor of this enormous patio. We finally found someone who had received the ballot in the mail. It was sent with no information. It was a ballot that used purely technical language, with no cover letter or background information of any sort. So we started a petitioning campaign to get signatures from people in the neighborhood, and we had more meetings, and we knocked on doors.

On that block where the patio had passed in a 7–5 vote according to the City, we got signatures from I would say something like 90 percent of the addresses, opposing the patio. We got over a hundred people to sign. Of the more than one hundred people we talked to, I would say the number who expressed their active support for the patio was between two and three.

30

We'd been talking to the councillor's office all this time, and we had what seemed to be a pretty compelling case that the polling on this patio issue was inaccurate, that we had forty really angry neighbors, as opposed to just me. We tried to convince him that the license for this patio should be denied, but the councillor didn't side with us. He talked about the importance of balancing the interests of business and the interests of residents. It seemed to us he was just waffling, refusing to take a side.

Meanwhile, the issuing date was coming up soon. Then, two days before the council hearing, I discovered a regulation that said you can't open a patio within twenty-five meters of a residence. And this patio was *next door* to my house and across a five-meter alley from an apartment.

It's weird, because Toronto is full of patios that are close to residences, and to this day I don't understand what the effect of that regulation is. Anyhow, I called the councillor's office, and I said, *Look, we have a hundred and twenty people opposing this patio, which is only supposed to be issued a license if there's popular support. The evidence for popular support is that supposedly seven people voted for it. We have signed letters from four of those seven people saying that they believe they voted for it based on misinformation. And furthermore, it's against the law to open a patio there to begin with.*

At this point, the councillor could no longer deny the force of our argument. He told us that if we wanted him to, he would oppose the patio in council. We'd won.

Then something funny happened. I was of course incredibly happy and really relieved, and also a tiny bit sad and a tiny bit worried. For all that I'd fought with the owners of the bar, I didn't feel like they were terrible people, you know? They had a hard time keeping their DJs under control, and they were trying to run a new business, and I'm not saying it was right for them to do what they did, but I didn't wish them ill. I felt bad for them.

The patio was a huge part of the owners' business plan, and I also realized I might be living next door to someone who felt I'd destroyed his business.

The day of the council hearing, I was there and the bar owners were there, and some of the bar staff, and some people from the Residents' Association were there. The meeting started, and before our matter came up, one of the people from the councillor's office came up to me and said, *The councillor wants to see if we can come to a compromise.*

And I felt furious. I thought, *Screw you. We've won!*

But we all went into his office—the bar staff, the residents— and something really remarkable happened. He said, *Look— you neighbors, you're upset because this bar plays loud music late at night with its doors open, and that causes you all sorts of problems, and you want that to stop. And you—the bar owners— you really, really want this patio. So maybe we can work something out where you, the neighbors, you let these guys have a patio that's a smaller patio than the bar asked for. You neighbors, do you care whether they have a patio that's open at dinnertime?* And we said no. Then he said to the bar owners, *What do you want from the patio?* The owners said, *We want to do a strong dinner business there.* He said to the bar owners, *Look—if the residents let you have a patio that closes at eleven and which is smaller than what you're asking for, would you be willing to promise that you'll keep the music down—not just when the patio's open, but all the time?* They said sure.

Everyone's initial response heading into the room was basically, *Fuck you, councillor.* The guys who owned the bar felt strongly that they had already jumped through all the hoops they had to jump through to get their patio. It had been approved at every level, had passed in this stupid vote, and they were completely entitled to this thing the councillor was trying to take away from them. Our feeling was that we'd won—they had promised us that we had won—and now they were trying to take this away from us. But the councillor was really emphatic and really insistent that a compromise could be had, and bit by bit it became clear that he was right that we would be better off with the deal he was proposing than if we blocked the patio altogether.

If we simply blocked the patio, all the existing problems with the bar would continue: they would likely continue to play loud music every night, even though they oughtn't to according to the unenforceable noise bylaw. I figured that, realistically, they would be less inclined to take our concerns into account, as they would see us as enemies and would have nothing more to lose by pissing us off—*and* I'd get to live next door to a business whose owners hated me. On the other hand, if we gave them a small patio, the cost to us was actually pretty minimal, because no one thought that a patio open at seven, eight, or nine o'clock was going to be very disruptive. In exchange, we could get the owners to agree to all kinds of conditions, and there would be a mechanism for enforcement, because if they failed to meet the conditions, they could lose their patio license.

So, in fact, this compromise was a *better* outcome than the victory we had imagined for ourselves. And that stayed with me forever. I think it's an incredible lesson. The fact that something can be *better than winning* in an apparently antagonistic situation like this one seems so important. Equally important is the ease with which you can mistake damage to the other party for advantage to yourself. We were so angry at the bar owners that we wanted to make sure they didn't gain an inch on their patio application, when in truth, their being open for dinner is, if anything, probably advantageous for us all. But we were just so embroiled in trying to stop their late-night business that we were blinded to that fact.

Sitting there in the councillor's office, we wrote a fairly painstakingly detailed set of conditions for this patio license. The license was conditional on their being better neighbors in a dozen different ways. They could no longer play music with the doors or windows open. They had to keep their music to levels where it couldn't be heard in the adjoining apartments, including mine. They had to hire staff to discourage their customers from yelling and screaming. They had to have regular meetings with their neighbors to stay on top of the issues. And a whole bunch of other little things. I think there were something like sixteen conditions in the license. It was a complicated document. But we were able to write it in about twenty minutes because we'd all been thinking about this stuff so much.

And it worked! It took a while for it to work, and at first it wasn't easy to get all the conditions enforced. It took a few months. But now I never hear music from the bar. Crowds of smokers gather outside their doors, which still creates pretty serious problems for the people who live next door to the patio, but that would've been the case regardless. They never play loud music that you can hear across the street. And for them, their patio is pretty successful, and their business is doing well.

In all these conversations, one thing the owners had always maintained was that they had no interest in the bar being as loud as it was, and friends of mine now tell me that their customers generally complained that their music was too loud. The hard thing, it turns out, was controlling the DJs, who aren't bar staff. So, really, it turns out that the quieter music levels in the bar don't even feel like a compromise to the bar owners and their customers. Everyone prefers it this way.

The Residents' Association still exists. New bars open in our neighborhood all the time. And we're a lot better at working with the bar owners to figure out how they can be good neighbors. But having so many bars in the neighborhood does make it really hard to live in. There are some people who own bars who are mad at me, though they're in the minority—most of them are pretty nice. The neighborhood is also now filled with guys in suits peeing in doorways, and people yelling and screaming, and people leaving trash all over and stealing my newspaper and putting garbage in my bike basket. And they feel like real invaders sometimes. There's a sort of class component, too, in that the people who come to drink in our neighborhood tend to be richer young people from other neighborhoods. It sometimes feels like they come to slum in our neighborhood, the badlands where you can behave inappropriately.

12. There Are Some Games
I Won't Play with My Friends

Starting a few years ago, a bunch of my friends started playing a game called Mafia. It is a game played by about fifteen people in a circle. Three of the people are Mafia members who kill other players, and it's up to the rest of the group to figure out who those three are through a process of questioning.

When people are playing Mafia, they get into really impassioned arguments and accusations. To win at the game, you need to be really good at convincing people that other people are lying, and convincing people that you're telling the truth when you're not.

My friends played it pretty regularly, but I only ever played the game once. I was a Mafia member, and I won by convincing everybody that I wasn't one. I thought, *Why would I ever want to play this game again?* Partly I just didn't want to ruin my perfect record, but partly it seemed like a really self-defeating sort of victory. If you're really good at charades, your friends might end up thinking, *Wow, this person is really good at communicating things or at understanding what other people are trying to convey, even in difficult situations.* But when you win at Mafia, people just think, *Wow, that person is really good at convincing me that they're being honest when in fact they are lying.* Why would I want my friends to think that about me?

13. Social Music

Over the past hundred years or so, music has become a much less social experience for a lot of people. Music used to be something you did, something you made with the people around you. Now, for many people, it's something made by skilled professionals you have never met, that you listen to as a largely passive audience, often at a substantial spatial and temporal distance from the performance.

Don't get me wrong, I *love* the present-day mediascape. I'm not calling for a return to the good old days. I think it's *amazing* that we all have instant access to a universe of music, all the time. But there's also something exciting about the dimension of music that's social, that's about making it together.

I run a series called Terrible Noises for Beautiful People, which is pretty much all about the question: *What sorts of aesthetically interesting experiences can you give to an audience by having them choose sounds and make sounds together, rather than by having them listen to sounds chosen by and made by someone else?* Some of the Terrible Noises events are structured as classes, some are more like participatory events—performances where all the sounds are made by the audience.

During these events, people are able to derive a lot of aesthetic pleasure from the very simplest group exercises. You get a roomful of people and you ask them to close their eyes and make and hold a vowel sound together. And you know what? It sounds *amazing*! I mean, it's the most boring, unmusical sound you can imagine—a couple of dozen people holding an unpitched drone. But when you're *in* it, when you are doing it with people, it can be very beautiful and very interesting. There's lots of reasons for this, but the one I'm most interested in is that people have so little opportunity to enjoy the social component of music that doing an exercise like this stimulates a part of our musical enjoyment that's really underused—the part that just enjoys making sounds with other people.

I'm really interested in weaving the social and the musical together. I do a game called converge/diverge where people move toward a unison where everyone is making the same sound, then move back out toward increased difference, then move back in again toward convergence. The challenge of that piece is not only musical, it's social—how can a large group of people collectively choose a single sound to make? It's a hard thing do, and it calls into question all kinds of things about leadership, compromise, listening, and individuality.

Tension and resolution are basic ideas in music. If someone sings half a melody and stops in the middle, even if you've never heard the melody before, you'll know that that's not the end and it will sound dissatisfying. You know this because we have a set of rules about tension and resolution in music that mostly have to do with harmonic movement. A musical piece moves to a place of tension, which feels unstable or incomplete, then to resolution, which feels satisfying and done.

In the converge/diverge piece, tension in the game happens as disagreement, and resolution happens as agreement. Since the piece is meant to be listened to by the people who are playing the game, when you hear the sonic component of agreement or disagreement, you are also simultaneously experiencing it on a social level. I think the interaction between those levels—between the social interactions and the way you hear and create those sounds—is complicated and exciting and mysterious.

14. Manners

For a while, I wrote a manners column for a magazine. On one level, manners is really just a tiny little subset of ethics. What having good manners is about is not making yourself more important than other people, which is what most ethics is about. People know that kind of instinctively.

I think manners also specifically end up being about a couple of other things: rules and communication. Things become a lot easier when people have shared standards of what's expected, and a lot more complicated when people don't.

The famous example of this in ethics is the rule that says you drive on the right-hand side of the road. No one imagines that there's some way in which driving on the right-hand side of the road is inherently better than driving on the left-hand side, but it's tremendously important that everyone agrees on the side, even though the rule is arbitrary. Manners work that way, too. People get pissed off at each other when one person has one set of expectations in their head and the other person has another. So, for instance, if everyone thinks a guest at a dinner party is obliged to bring a bottle of wine, things will work out okay. I'll bring wine to your place, you'll bring wine to my place. If I'm one of eight guests, we'll all bring wine. But if I exist in a social circle where half the people think bringing wine is the thing to do, and half the people don't, you're likely to end up with resentment, because some people will feel they're providing too much wine.

There's not really any reason for favoring one of these rules over the other. It's perfectly fine for it not to be an expectation for people to bring wine—that a host should provide everything for their guests and that that's what it means to be a host, and we all take turns being one. And of course it's fine the other way around. Mostly what matters is that there be agreement.

I actually think about this a lot with the Residents' Association. Occasionally people say, well, in Latin American countries people happily live in neighborhoods where people play music all night long, and there's none of this sense that you're obliged to protect your neighbors from noise.

And I guess what I think is that, yes, a culture like that can work. If I live in a culture where hearing other people's music and noise is the norm, then that's great. When I feel like listening to loud music late at night, I can do that. It's not that one attitude is necessarily better than the other, it's that we have to find one that's consistent and agreed upon. In general, I think the rule we tend to have in our culture is that it's not okay to make loud noise late at night, and if there's agreement on that rule, people can get along. But if there's not agreement, people feel resentful—not only because they don't like to hear loud noises at night, but because they feel bound by the other side of the agreement, which is that they're not allowed to make loud noises late at night.

By and large, contemporary society tends not to be a society with an incredible number of stated formal rules for behavior. We can use whatever fork we want for our salad and we don't use formal terms of address very often. The rules tend to be tacit and open-ended. We also tend to move between circles where the rules—tacit and open-ended as they are—change.

When I wrote my manners column, a lot of the time the question posed would be, *I think this, my friend thinks that, who's right?* And it's funny because often no one's right. If my friend thinks she should drive on the right-hand side of the road and I think I should drive on the left and there's no existing rule, no side is right. What matters is that there's agreement. I guess if I were a more influential manners columnist, I could be the person to establish these norms. But in the end, most of the advice

I ended up giving people was to try to talk to the other people involved.

Once, I was asked about when it's okay *not* to give up your seat in the subway. Manners dictate that the other person go first; that you give up your seat. But sometimes you're really tired and you've had a hard day and you're carrying something heavy and you really want to sit and you think the seat would serve you better than the other person. Can you slip ahead and take that seat? they asked.

The answer I gave, which I was really happy with, was: Ask them for it. Say to them, *I've had a really long day and I'm exhausted and would it be okay if I sat down?* Because, first of all, you're using direct communication. Also, you're letting them give it to you. You're being polite, which in terms of etiquette means a bunch of things. First, to let someone give something to you, you have to let them own it first. And you're letting it be their choice. In the first instance, where you push ahead and take their seat, they'll feel like, *Oh, some asshole stole a seat from me.* But in asking for the seat, if you do it right, they'll feel like a good person because they did a favor for a nice stranger.

15. How to Improvise,
and How Not to Not Improvise

There are a few things people do when they improvise. The worst attitude toward improvising—or the one that's least interesting to me—is to see it as a parlor trick, where you improvise by trying to be as prepared as you possibly can be for the various situations that might arise.

When I did theater improv, we would do scenes in different genres. You ask the audience for genre and they say, *Do a western!* or *Do a sci-fi!* It was understood that a good improviser would study the conventions of the genre and try to identify some of the clichés.

Then the audience would say, *Look at how skilled these people are! You can throw anything at them and they can handle anything well!* But for the improviser, that means you're prepared—not that you're improvising. The audience gives you a genre and you think, *Oh great! I'm ready for this!* But wouldn't it be more interesting and fun to think, *How great! I've never thought about this before. I'm surprised by this suggestion!*

The idea that improvisers would eliminate surprise from their own experience goes against my ideas about what's interesting about improvisation as a practice—and I'm much more interested in improvisation as a practice, or as something to do, than as something for people to watch.

Why would someone go to see an improv show? What I began to feel as a performer after a while was, *Maybe if we really cared about our audience, we'd write something for them beforehand.*

Otherwise it's just a display of skill—which is the *most boring* kind of art. The audience sits there and thinks, *Wow, it sure is impressive that they made up something on the spot which is almost as funny as it would have been if they'd written it before!*

The idea that the point of art is to be impressive is—to me—*incredibly* distressing. Skill should be a means to an end, or it becomes like watching acrobatics, or being very tall. There's a subset of guitar geeks who like to watch people perform very difficult guitar solos. They think, *Wow! That guy sure can play fast and play complicated chord changes!* But is that better than someone who can create a well-crafted song with subtlety?

You go to watch a smart person talk because they might have things to say to you that would be interesting, not so you can come away thinking, *Wow, that's a smart person!* It depresses me for the audience that it would think, *Look how much better that person is than me.* That doesn't mean performers can't be great. In some cases, excellence is a means to an end. A great novelist can create a great book which has value, but that excellence is a means to that end, whereas with something like juggling, that's all it is: amazement that a person can do that. At a certain level, virtuosity has only one thing to say, and that is: *Look at how good I am.*

In improv, being a virtuoso theater improviser involves knowing the conventions in all sorts of different film genres so you can call upon them when needed, and being able to do lots of different accents. Then there's *real* virtuosity, which is being able to handle an unexpected turn in a way that's quick and witty, being able to build a scene out of surprising elements.

But, ultimately, none of that is really what interests me about improvisation.

I'm interested in improv as an experience for people to *have*, a thing for people to *do*, a practice.

When I was in college, I auditioned for the improv group at

school but didn't get in. I figured the easiest way to be in a group would be to start my own group, so I did that. I wasn't particularly interested in being the leader of that group. I figured we'd work collaboratively and that out of necessity I would teach them the basics of improv.

That's not what happened. What happened was I really liked teaching and they really liked me being the teacher. I let everybody who wanted to join, join. And it was a fucked-up bunch of people; some were very skilled, some were shy. We had three rehearsals a week, and we did a show every week. We did this for three or four years. It was serious, and we did pretty well for a student group.

After I left school, I kept trying to re-create that experience, but I always hated it, and I hated watching other groups. I think what took me a long time to figure out—and which I only figured out years later—is that the thing we were providing for our audience was not the really valuable part. The really valuable experience was the experience that people in the group were having. The experience that I was providing the *group* was in fact the experience that I *hoped* we were providing to the *audience*, but were not.

So I started to think about whether I could do theater and art that would consist of getting people to *do* this improv-type stuff rather than watch it.

Keith Johnstone, who pretty much invented the sort of theater improv I'm interested in, has a book called *Impro*, which I've been reading and rereading for over twenty years and which explains his ideas about improv, and teaching, and everything else. In that book, Johnstone talks about doing all sorts of things in workshops with his students and finding it all hysterically funny. They wanted to take it onstage to test it, to see if it really *was* as funny as they thought.

For me, I think, *Oh, what an interesting mistake!* The way people laugh when they're taking an improv class together—the quality of laughter is so incredible and deep and real and serious. And it always feels to me that, in a way, comedy shows and funny movies are attempts to create a bottled version of that—of what happens with your friends when you're laughing and joking around. But to make the mistake of thinking that the bottled version is primary and the *interpersonal* version is the thing to doubt—to say that it's only real if you bottle and perform it— means you imagine yourself to be in the making-people-laugh business.

So one way to think about improv is: we're going to train improvisers to make the audience laugh, and they're going to laugh in the same way as people who sit in movies laugh. But I became very excited to think I was in the business of making people laugh by having them joke around with *each other*. So now people pay me money and they run around. They make the stuff together. And there's no audience.

So what is true improv?

I guess the biggest thing is that it's actually about letting yourself be surprised and letting yourself be off-balance. One approach is to develop as many tools as you can so you're never off-balance, but the approach I'm interested in is to develop skills so you can respond well to being off-balance, and especially so you can enjoy being off-balance.

A lot of people are scared to be surprised, I find. And a lot of things I don't like in improv come down to people's attempts to avoid that surprise. But a real part of what it means to truly improvise is to *really* not know where you're going, to *really* not know what you're doing. There's a feeling I associate with improvising which I think is a really thrilling feeling, which is the feeling of being at once very comfortable and yet having no idea what's going to happen. That's thrilling, and it's a little mysterious, and there's pleasure in feeling out of control. There's a real joy in starting a sentence and not knowing how it's going to finish.

45

16. The Crazy Parts

A lot of contemporary clinical psychology for mental disorders consists of a catalogue of the kinds of intellectual mistakes people make when they're crazy. I think having an awareness of that catalogue of mistakes is tremendously helpful, in the same way that you teach people the fallacies when you study philosophy.

So, for instance: Washing your hands regularly is a good thing to do to reduce your risk of catching a cold. Some people wash their hands a thousand times a day because no amount of hand-washing is sufficient to ensure that they won't get a cold. It's an intellectual mistake, a logical fallacy: you can't totally eliminate colds through hours of hand-washing. I think there's a lot to learn from these kinds of mistakes.

I guess I think it's normal for people to be a little bit crazy in a million different ways. We all go through spells when we really irrationally berate or underevaluate ourselves, which is what people with depression do. It's natural for everyone, at times, to get a thought stuck in their head, or to have a hard time stopping working on something far past the point when it's useful, which is what happens to people with obsessive-compulsive disorder. It's normal, too, for our minds to overascribe meaning to random or meaningless occurrences, which is what happens much more dramatically in people with schizophrenia.

Sometimes we can tell what our slightly crazy parts are. By definition, a phobia is actually a phobia only insofar as you recognize it as irrational—otherwise it's a psychotic delusion. So, for instance, if the sight of a rubber duck makes you very uncomfortable every time you see one, and you think that's nuts, that's a phobia. If, however, you think it's going to hurt you, then it's a delusion.

The challenge is to figure out what parts of your thoughts and feelings are irrational. Sometimes it's not obvious, so you have to pay close attention to what you're thinking. That's a skill, and you need to step back from these thoughts at a time when you're not emotionally engaged with them.

So, for instance, I *really* don't think I have obsessive-compulsive disorder as a medical or psychological condition, but I certainly think there are elements of my personality that resemble some of the traits of that condition sometimes. I'm definitely sometimes inclined to put more energy than is necessary into attaining certainty when certainty is actually impossible, or when the benefit of extra certainty would be quite low.

It's a funny paradox that one of the main things I do is teach people to improvise. I teach people, specifically, *not* to plan ahead, to be okay with not knowing what's coming next, to *hope* to be surprised—but in the grand scheme of my life, I'm not very good at any of those things. Compared with most people, I think I worry a fair bit. I'm inclined to need control. I structure my time very carefully in a calendar.

I don't think there's a contradiction there. If I were really good at being spontaneous in my day-to-day life, that sort of spontaneity wouldn't seem so remarkable to me. I likely wouldn't feel inclined to think about it so much. I probably wouldn't find it such an interesting thing to try to teach it to people in the context of improvisation.

17. Charging for My Classes

I keep changing how I price my classes because the things I want are sort of contradictory. On the one hand, I want to make money. On the other hand, I want lots of people to come, and I want to have a nice mix of people. I don't want the classes to be only for people who can afford a really expensive leisure activity. I used to have a sliding scale where I would charge less for students or artists, or I would have a regular rate and then have a reduced rate for people in financial need. But now I just name a price: "$360 or whatever you want." And I let people choose whatever price they want to pay. It's not a great socialist or antimaterialist gesture or anything. It's just a lot less hassle and headache for me.

A lot of the people who *do* have money who take my classes specifically like the idea of taking a class where there are artists and writers, so I try to explain to them that if they're paying a little more, then they're subsidizing that experience. It works out pretty well. Everyone's usually pretty comfortable with what they pay, and a surprising number of people choose to pay the full amount. Occasionally but infrequently people choose to pay more than the asking price. Sometimes people are unemployed when they start taking the class and then they find a job and then they'll pay me extra money at the end of the class.

Amid all this, though, I'm also a real stickler about payments. If people drop out of the class, I usually won't refund their money. People are allowed to pay in installments, but they have to give me postdated checks up front. So there is a contract and the contract is binding, it's just up to that person to choose what the terms of the contract are.

People drop out of the classes for different reasons. Sometimes people drop out after the first class because they hate it, and sometimes I'll refund their money in those cases, though I do not advertise the fact. Sometimes people drop out because their lives get too busy. This often happens with people who have chosen to pay the full amount, probably because there's some correlation between having money and having a busy schedule. In those cases I don't refund.

18. What Is a Game?

A game has rules, it has goals, it has at least one player and a beginning and an end, there are elements of it that are arbitrary, and there has to be something about it that's not real.

What I often do when I get frustrated is I think of something as a game. With neighborhood activism, I might think to myself, *It's a video game. There are patterns on my screen*—in this case emails—*and I'm trying to get certain patterns to come about and certain patterns to not come about.*

Looking at it that way means you don't need to get as upset if you fail. You can approach challenges in a happier spirit. You can be more effective—in part because you're more effective when you're not upset. You don't need to feel angry toward your opponent, because in a sport or a game, the other person is *necessarily* trying to do the opposite thing from you. That doesn't make them a bad person.

19. Spam

I spend more time than I care to admit thinking about spam. I've had the same email address for well over ten years and have never been careful about publishing it, so it's on websites and in newsgroups and I use it to sign up for things, so it's on pretty much every spam list in the world. But it's a cool email address so I like to keep it. It's misha@web.net. I worry that if I use a new email address people who used to know me won't be able to reach me anymore.

This address receives around eight hundred spam messages a day on average, so spam filtering is very important to me. I've spent lots of time configuring different systems, and I frequent the forums of my email provider, to look for tips on spam filtering but more often to answer questions that other people have about it.

The best spam filtering software available, as far as I know, is SpamAssassin. It's open source, it gets updated a lot, people can add their own rules. But the best thing about SpamAssassin is that it tries to use as many different methods as possible to determine whether a message is spam. It does a gazillion different tests on a message, and each of those tests has a score, and then all the scores are added up, and then SpamAssassin will do something subtle like put a little header in the message that says, *This message got a 7.3 spam score*. Then you can decide what to do with the messages based on that score. That's really, really important for me.

No spam-sorting method is completely perfect, and that means that any method will either determine that some legitimate messages are spam or will determine that some spam messages are legitimate or usually both. That's why places like Hotmail or Gmail, rather than deleting spam altogether, put messages in a spam folder. The idea is that you ought to check your spam folder occasionally to make sure that no legitimate messages found their way in there.

But if there are eight hundred messages a day in your spam folder, you can't really do that. So I sort my email into a few different levels. Messages that look like they're pretty much definitely spam all go into their own "almost definitely spam" folder. I never look in that folder unless there's a specific message that I fear might have gone missing and I know what I'm looking for. In two years, I think there's been one legitimate message that's ever ended up in there, and it wasn't a very important one.

Messages that are pretty much definitely not spam go straight into my inbox. And messages that look like they might be spam go into my inbox but with a tag next to them, which makes it really easy to sort and find them. The number per day varies a lot, because spam is a constant arms race between the methods the spammers use and the updates to spam software, so depending on the season, I'll get anywhere from one or two a day to maybe twenty when things are really bad, but I can deal with twenty identified potential spam messages. It's a system that works pretty well for me.

With computer security, there are all sorts of measures taken to minimize the risks of different kinds of damage, but the damage that's often overlooked is the damage caused by the measures themselves. So, for instance, when you get locked out of your email because you forgot your password or because your email service is worried that someone else got your password and locks you out—that's real damage. All the time one wastes keeping track of passwords and forgetting them and losing them and getting locked out of accounts and all that—those are real security costs.

People talk about trying to find the solution that blocks the most spam, but the trick isn't to block the *most* spam, it's to block the most spam while blocking the fewest legitimate messages. I mean, it's easy to make a filter that blocks all your spam and just won't let any of your messages through at all. In fact, with my email—and I think this is true for most people—the spam filter isn't blocking spam, it's actually doing the opposite. It's looking at the thousand or so messages a day that come into my email inbox, 90 percent of which are garbage, and trying to pluck out the small minority that are actually legitimate email. So you really have to think about it that way.

On all the discussion forums for FastMail, people are always suggesting new rules. For instance, they notice that a lot of their spam is in Russian, so they figure if they block all the emails with Russian characters, they'll block more spam. But every new rule that you add introduces a very real possibility of blocking more legitimate mail.

This actually had very real consequences for me with the Residents' Association, working on some really political and time-sensitive emails. After a couple of days, it turned out I was completely out of the loop. An overzealous system administrator had instituted a new spam filter. The bar we were talking about was called the Cock and Tail, and every email with *cock* in the subject line was silently being deleted.

By far the coolest part of SpamAssassin—and it's used in a lot of other spam filters, too—is something called Bayesian filtering. Bayesian filtering is a kind of deal you strike with your spam filter, because as a user you have some responsibility. Your responsibility is that you have to tell your spam filter which of your incoming messages are legitimate mail and which ones are spam. There are lots of things that make that easy to do, say, by designating folders for spam and legitimate mail, but one way or another you have to let the server know.

Then the server can do this awesome thing: it can statistically analyze the messages you get and look for patterns that distinguish the spam from legitimate messages. The more mail

53

you train it on, the more accurate it becomes. The really fantastic thing about this is that it learns. A lot of people understand this as meaning that the filter can keep up with the latest techniques spammers use, which is true to some degree, but more important, it learns what *your* email looks like. So the classic example is that if you're, say, a pharmacist, the word *Viagra* might actually appear in your legitimate mail and the Bayesian filter would learn that, so even though *Viagra* is a spam trigger for most people, it wouldn't be for you.

The Bayesian filter points out that mail to me should *look like my mail*. My mail usually includes the names of some of my friends or coworkers. It often includes the names of streets and places in Toronto, the names of projects that I'm working on, and words associated with them. The Bayesian filter will learn all of these words automatically, and the really great thing is that spammers, no matter how smart they get—unless they actually start hacking into my account or the accounts of my friends— though they might be able to know the features that distinguish spam from legitimate mail in general, they can't really learn the features that make my mail look like my mail.

20. Margaux

I live with Margaux Williamson. We've lived together for quite a few years now. We're very happy together.

For a long time in my life, I didn't have serious girlfriends that much. It was something that in the abstract I always thought I should do.

I had certain ideas about what kind of person my girlfriend might be. I met Margaux and I was pretty fascinated by her. She's a remarkably unusual person. She doesn't really think like anyone else. She doesn't really act like anyone else.

I was with her for a while and I kept thinking, *This is so not like the person I'd imagined.* And at the same time I thought, once the relationship got at all serious, *Well, I'm kind of stuck, because there's no way in the world that I'm going to be able to find someone who's sort of like Margaux but better, because there's no one like Margaux.*

I love Margaux tremendously, and I'm very happy to have her in my life. There's no way I could have seen her coming. It's not like there was this Margaux-shaped hole in my life. There's no way on earth that I could have invented her. She's just too unusual. She came as a real surprise.

I think the way I'd always thought this sort of thing worked was that you had some sort of imaginary person in your head and then you'd meet someone who was pretty close to that imaginary person, but it turns out that what worked for me was meeting a person who didn't correspond to anything in my head at all but was something new that came from the world.

21. Charades Homework

In my classes, we strictly adhere to the tournament regulations of charades. To the best of my knowledge, there are no charade tournaments, so I'm free to invent these regulations as I see fit. When some people play charades, they use hand signals to indicate the letters of the alphabet. Tournament regulations forbid this. Tournament regulations are also very strict about any talking when acting out the charade. You can't say, *Whoa, this one's hard* or *Yes, yes, you're on the right track.*

It seems kind of important to me that there really are probably no tournaments for charades. It's a game that has built into it a certain limit to how seriously you can take it, because you could just use sign language and you'd win. One of the things I try to teach people is that, on one level, the goal of charades is to convey a clue to another person as quickly as possible under a certain set of constraints. Really, though, the goal of charades is to amuse people.

The most important gesture in charades is the gesture for "the whole thing," which involves drawing your hands in a big sweeping gesture through the air. This means you're actually going to act out the movie or book itself, rather than individual words in the title. This strategy is often the most fun.

HOMEWORK

Sometimes in class people will get a really hard clue to act out, and they'll object, *Oh, this is impossible. We can't do this one.*

I don't believe that, so I will have them work on the hardest possible clues. We do this as a two-part homework assignment. For the first part, I ask people to go home and think up the hardest possible charades clues they can and to bring to class ten to twenty really insanely hard ones. Then we'll shuffle them up and everyone takes home a random selection of the hardest possible clues that anyone in class could think up, and everyone is given a week to think about them. Then they come back to class with their incredibly hard clues after the week of strategizing.

I've already told them to think about the fact that charades acting is a dialogue, so they can't just come in with one idea and act it out and expect it to work. They need to have a few strategies ready and be prepared to adapt. The last time we did this, people really took that instruction to heart, and they came in and we were able to guess them all. I was pretty happy.

HARD CLUES

Some people who play charades think that a hard, fun clue might be a title of a book that no one's heard of, but I think that's stupid and wrong. There's an *infinite* number of book and song titles that people haven't heard of. If you want to make the clues hard in that way, why not make every clue just be a random series of words? What makes clues fun, for the purpose of the game, is recognition—is thinking, *Oh, what's that? What's a movie whose third word is "war"?* It's fun if the title is something a guesser has to dig up from their brain's dusty corners, but it should still be recallable.

Genuinely hard clues are hard because there are lots of individual words that are hard to act out. There was one clue that no one in a certain class could guess, and it was, at the time, a contemporary Margaret Atwood novel that more than half the people in the class had heard of. The book was *Oryx and Crake*.

the Symbionese Liberation Army

Sum 41

"The more things change, the more they stay the same."

Guam

Being and Nothingness

Sometimes a Great Notion

the Dutch tulip craze of the seventeenth century

Fletch

Søren Kierkegaard

Bob and Carol and Ted and Alice

the Koran

"Bootylicious"

"The square of the hypotenuse is equal to the sum of the squares
of the two adjacent sides."

E Pluribus Unum

Vinnie Barbarino

Koyaanisqatsi

Troilus and Cressida

the lambada

1984

Radical Chic & Mau-Mauing the Flak Catchers

Mr. Snuffleupagus

"It is a truth universally acknowledged, that a single man in pos-
session of a good fortune, must be in want of a wife."

"Que Sera, Sera"

Eine Kleine Nachtmusik

Gödel, Escher, Bach

Soylent Green

shock and awe

The Metamorphosis

" 'Twas brillig, and the slithy toves did gyre and gimble in the
wabe."

trickle-down economics

22. Harvard and Class

I grew up in Montreal and I went to an upper-middle-class Jewish day school where kids had parents who maybe owned a carpet store or maybe were dentists. And then I went to Harvard for college. And it was pretty weird.

When I applied, I thought it would be great because I would get to meet lots of smart people. Those were the kinds of people I liked to be friends with and I thought there would be more of them there. That was the main reason I thought it would be a fun place to be. I don't think I was super-ambitious or professional-minded or even a very good student.

The thing I figured out soon after I applied was that, on *Gilligan's Island*, it wasn't the Professor who went to Harvard, it was Mr. Howell—the rich man. That was something of a revelation.

It's funny, because what a lot of people talk about when they talk about going to Harvard is being really intimidated by the place when they arrive. I wasn't at all intimidated by the place when I arrived—but I was really intimidated after graduating.

I arrived at Harvard from Montreal, which is a pretty fucking hip place to be an eighteen-year-old. I'd been going to bars for a while, and I was in a political theater company that did shows in lofts with homeless people and South American activists. And we went to pubs and got old gay men to buy us drinks. It was a pretty cool, fun, and exciting life for a kid in Montreal. It was a very vibrant place, and young people were really part of the life of the city.

Then when I went to Harvard, the place was full of these

nominally smart, interesting people, all of whom at the age of eighteen seemed perfectly happy to live in dormitories and be on a meal plan and live a fully institutional life. And that was completely maddening! This was the opposite of everything I'd hoped for from the environment I'd be in.

By design, the university wants to be an enclosed institution, so you're very strongly required to live on campus, which means that you're not living in the city. You don't have a landlord or neighbors or those kinds of things. You're pretty much required to sign up for the meal plan, which means you don't interact with people in restaurants or grocery stores or any of that kind of stuff. The drinking age is twenty-one, and it's strictly enforced in the city but mostly unenforced on campus, which means if you want to drink or go to a party, you can only do that on campus, but if you want to go see a band at a club, you can't do that.

I spent my first year trying to figure out how to participate in the life of the city in some way, but by the end of my first year I think I gave up because the pull of the university community was so strong and the boundaries were so hard to overcome.

By the end of university, I ended up living somewhere that was considered "off campus"—a place called the Dudley Co-op. The Dudley Co-op was located in a building that was owned by Harvard. About thirty or forty Harvard students lived there. We did our own cooking and cleaning, but we were on the university phone system and the university did the building maintenance, yet it was considered off campus. That's how fully institutionalized life at Harvard was: even Dudley House, which was the organization that looked after off-campus living, provided university-owned accommodation for people who wanted to live off campus.

There actually was a small percentage of students who genuinely did live off campus—like 1 percent—but you had to get university permission. I think the explanation the university would give is that going to Harvard isn't just a set of courses, it's an experience and a community, and they're interested in people being part of that community, which means living there and participating in what they call the "house system," which are the different dorms students live in.

But the end result is that it makes the university into an ivory tower—I mean, *incredibly* so. It would be one thing if you were out in the woods—but this is *Boston*. In four years of living in that city I pretty much didn't come to know *anybody* who wasn't affiliated with Harvard. And I'm someone who's interested in cities, and who's interested in meeting different kinds of people. The university is a completely isolated environment, and the fact that you're inside a city somehow makes that more insidious and terrible.

All the parties were on campus. So when you went to a party—and that's what you would do Friday and Saturday night, you would go to a party—the party would be on campus, which means, sort of implicitly, that if you're a student at the university, you're welcome, and if you're not, you're trespassing. So even at parties—and I went to parties for four years—the average number of people at a given party who weren't Harvard students was zero. All of this serves to create a very weird, very contained environment.

When I was at university, it shocked me how focused so many people were about their careers, in ways that often seemed pretty narrow. I guess I knew that Harvard attracts very ambitious young people, but I was still surprised. In Montreal I knew a lot of really interesting people doing interesting things, and there was actually a lot less of that at Harvard than I would have expected. In retrospect it's not surprising. At a certain level, an institution like that is going to attract people who are very good at playing by the rules.

Of course there were many great people there, and I made

lots of great friends, but it was a weird, weird fucking place to be. If you were interested in biology, you could go to Stephen Jay Gould's office hours and talk to him. When I took a survey psychology course, the lecture on behaviorism was given by B. F. Skinner. I was on the staff of the *Harvard Lampoon*, where we'd do things like invite John Cleese to accept an award, and he'd come have dinner with the forty of us. George Plimpton would sometimes drop by unannounced. So really the most notable thing was just the social access.

Then, in terms of work possibilities, too—if you were someone on the *Lampoon*, and if you liked making jokes, then a very real job possibility you faced after graduation was to go write for *The Simpsons* in its third season or *Letterman*, at a time when these were the best shows on TV. Many people got book contracts while they were still in college, partly because if you go to Harvard, the eyes of the country are on you in a certain way. So if you want to write a book about taking Prozac and being slutty, that's not as marketable as a book about taking Prozac and being slutty at Harvard.

After I graduated, I moved cities a few times. I lived in Boston for a bit. I lived in London. I sort of thought about living in New York but it never quite worked out. I moved to Montreal. I ended up in Toronto.

Now, America really has an upper class, though they don't like to talk about it much. And class in America is pretty fluid, so people at Harvard really do come from different backgrounds. There are people there whose families have gone to Harvard for generations and who run the world, and there are people there from pretty middle-class backgrounds, and there are people there who are the first person in their family to go to college.

A thing that's very nice and very terrible is that those class differences are very rarely talked about at Harvard. So you might have some sort of movie image where the snobs are sort of looking down their noses at the poor kids, but the reality is that once you're at Harvard, no one's a poor kid anymore. You're all, instantly and at that moment, in one of the most privileged positions of the American upper class.

I did an event for my fifteen-year reunion called *Interviews with Harvard Alumni Who Feel Weird About Harvard*. It was based on a theater project that my friend Darren O'Donnell created—a wonderful show called *Q&A*. How *Q&A* works is this: Darren gets a bunch of people to sit in an audience in a theater and then, one by one, people are randomly chosen to sit onstage, and everyone in the audience can interview them and ask them questions. The rule is that the person onstage can refuse to answer any question. By its design, people are encouraged to ask difficult and uncomfortable questions. There are cameras on the people being interviewed, and their faces are projected on a big screen to make it more theatrical.

I proposed this project to my alumni association and I explained that I specifically wanted to get people who felt that the whole experience of going to Harvard was confusing or weird, and the alumni association was like, *Great*. I mean, they are such a classy organization. A lesser institution, I think, would be threatened, but Harvard booked me a lecture hall in the Science Center and set me up with a really good PA system, and we did this show.

Harvard has all the reunions at five-year intervals at the same time, so there are people who graduated five years ago, fifteen, twenty, all the way up to forty, forty-five years ago—and one by one these people got onstage and talked about all the stuff they couldn't or didn't talk about at the time. In five minutes they would say things they had not said in four whole years.

There was someone who was the first person in her town to go to Harvard, and she talked about how this completely tore her apart, and how the whole time she was at Harvard she always felt out of place and everyone treated her badly, but when she went home everyone thought she was stuck-up so she felt out of place at home, too. We had people who were fourth-generation Harvard people who talked about the pressures of *that* world. There was this African-American guy who described a kind of racism that had been invisible to all of us. When I was a student at Harvard, it felt like people barely talked about class or race. Those few hours felt really important.

So much of the world works around social networks. Harvard functions as a crossroads early in life through which the people who are going to be the most privileged people in America can meet each other and form social bonds. And it's nice in a way that there is a real effort to bring new people into that system. I *guess*. I suppose that a meritocratic elitism is a little better than a purely inherited or wealth-based elitism.

If you go to Harvard and then you live in New York, no matter what you do, the fact will remain that you will have old college friends who are in the top positions in whatever field of endeavor you're concerned with. If you're twenty-five, you'll know people who are getting their first pieces published in *The New Yorker*. If you're forty, you'll know people who are editors of *The New Yorker*. You will know people who are affiliated with every level of government. And across the board, just everywhere, you will know some people at the top of everything.

But in Canada, if you went to Harvard, it's just sort of a weird novelty, a strange fact about you, like that you're a member of Mensa or you have an extra thumb. There's no Harvard community here. There are sort of equivalent upper-class communities to some degree, like maybe people who went to Upper Canada College prep school, but it's not even remotely the same thing. I mean, partly there just aren't the same heights to aspire to. There's no equivalent to being the editor of *The New Yorker* in Canada, or being an American movie producer or anything like that. Partly, the advantages of class aren't as unevenly distributed in general.

So while going to Harvard constitutes a sort of invitation to join the American upper class, this invitation is pretty useless if you're living in Canada. I often think about how I was given this invitation—this tremendously valuable thing—and I just kind of threw it away. I'm not sure how I feel about this.

23. The Rocks Game

I went down to the lake the day I decided we'd play this game, and I got a huge bucket of rocks which I carried back on my bike. They were pretty heavy.

This game, which I sometimes play when I teach my music classes, can be played in groups of different sizes. It can work with groups of two people or five or six. You can also play this game at home with a friend—it's pretty easy—and you can play it at the beach. That's where Margaux taught it to me. I'm not sure where she learned it.

The game is this: Everyone gets some rocks. You take turns either placing a rock on the floor somewhere or moving a rock that's already there. It's sort of like that Uniqlo game. What's amazing and surprising is that this turns out to be a really interesting game. All kinds of stuff comes up. People start moving rocks together into one pattern and everyone might start to work toward that one pattern, then someone gets bored and does something else. People might appreciate this or be angry about it. People might fight each other or try to cooperate.

When playing the game, especially to teach music improvisation, I encourage people to try not to communicate in any way other than the movement and placement of these rocks. No talking or facial expressions or pointing.

So you're moving rocks, but by moving these rocks, you're also at the same time commenting on the movement of the rocks. You're expressing approval or disapproval of a set of patterns or gestures by how you respond to them with rocks. Aesthetics emerge very quickly. So when someone places a rock down, you might think, *Aha! Wasn't that a brilliant thing to do with a rock!* Or, *That ruins everything.* Or, *That was kind of boring.*

I like the way the game teaches something fundamental about music improvisation that can be hard to talk about otherwise. The stuff that happens in an abstract sound improvisation is very difficult to discuss, but with rocks you can literally point at them and everyone sees the same thing. The game provides really nice, genuinely physical, concrete illustrations of the sort of stuff that happens in music improvisation.

I think playing the game can make people smart about things like: what it means to participate in a pattern versus what it means to break a pattern; what it means to try to start a new pattern or to do something that's a counterpoint.

In order to enjoy the game—and all these games need to be enjoyed to be played properly—you need to figure out how to take pleasure in having limited control over what happens. If you want the patterns to unfold exactly as you want them to, you'll find the game frustrating. At the same time, if you have no attachment to the outcome, you'll find the game boring. The best thing is to have an intention, but also to be open to surprise.

24. Some Video on the Internet

One of the most dispiriting things about people, for me, is their capacity to be blinded by a sort of good-guy, bad-guy thinking. So if some individual or group becomes your enemy, then suddenly everything they do becomes suspect, whereas everything that your team does is okay.

There was this video floating around the Internet, where someone went around with a camera to McCain-Palin rallies and interviewed people with the goal of getting them to say pretty provocative things, and the questions were there—they were part of the tape—and you could hear them asking these provocative questions and trying to get people to say that Obama is a terrorist or to say things that sort of bordered on racism.

Then this video was cut together and put online, presumably to stir up outrage among Democrats. Now, to me, that video is just so infuriating and unfair. I mean, what does it really tell us? That among McCain supporters there are some people that are stupid? Is that really surprising? I'm sure there are plenty of stupid people among Democrats, and there are stupid Greens, and there are plenty of stupid feminists, and stupid libertarians, and stupid Communists, and stupid people who believe in evolution, and stupid people who believe in Christianity. Pretty much any ideology and point of view is populated by at least some stupid people. It's not that surprising to learn that there are some dumb, racist people in America, and even less surprising to learn that those people support the white candidate over the black one. But what does that tell us? Is there really anything wrong with McCain for having dumb people among his supporters?

The really dispiriting part was seeing this posted on Meta-Filter, which is this online forum that I like to read in large part because it always seems to be populated by fairly reasonable, intelligent people. I looked through the comments on Meta-Filter, and pretty much everybody agreed with each other, expressing their moral outrage and disgust at the McCain rally, making great gestures of their tremendous despair for the country—that the electoral process had sunk so low.

Mostly, people on MetaFilter are Democrats. And there's no question in my mind that had there been a video where some right-wing reporter went out and found the stupidest, most extreme, most lunatic supporters of Obama and strung together a video of them, everyone on the forum would have been furious at the videographer. But here, somehow, people couldn't see that.

This just makes me nuts about people. It's as though there's this part of the human brain that allows us to perceive the moral failings and intellectual shortcomings of our enemies *so clearly*—often even in cases where they don't even exist—while at the same time being blind to the moral failings and intellectual shortcomings of our friends.

25. People Who Take My Classes

Graduate students
Musicians
People who work at ad agencies
People who take a lot of workshops
Fans of Trampoline Hall
A surprising number of high school teachers
College professors
Quakers

26. Shut Up and Listen

It's *amazing* to me that someone can have the courage to write a book or to stand up onstage and talk for a long time. It just seems impossible to imagine that what you have to say might be so important that other people would want to sit down and listen to it or take time out of their life to read it.

So this book is a weird project for me. There's all this stuff that's in my head that I think about. It's not easy for me to imagine that it could be interesting to anyone else.

Margaux and I had an argument about this, watching some terrible monologues being performed at some club in New York. I was so angry and outraged that they thought that it was fair to make the demand, *I'm going to talk now and you all have to shut up and listen.* I told Margaux, *You have to be really sure that what you are saying is worthwhile and good before you ask that of people.*

She thought I was wrong. She thought that to do any kind of art, you need to be willing to have people pay attention to it, and you don't know whether it's going to be any good. If the contract is that you have to be absolutely certain that it's going to be worth people's while, nobody would do anything. No one's forcing people to shut up and listen.

I think she's probably right, but I can't help feeling this way.

27. Is Monogamy a Trick?

When I was younger, I thought that monogamy was a trick. It was a trick that society played on people to make them serve the needs of global capital better—to domesticate or tame the real pleasures of sex, to make people into better workers and consumers. I guess my evidence for this at the time was just that there was so much about the idea of monogamy that didn't make sense. I spent a lot of time learning about different kinds of open relationships, but in the end there were many things about open relationships that didn't make sense either. I think the truth is that any individual has a wild number of desires and needs and fears about sex and intimacy and wanting to take care of someone and wanting to be taken care of, and within any one person there's a lot of contradictory desires. Then, between any two people the number of contradictions among those desires is just squared.

So anything you do is going to be fucked-up. And I think it's really easy, with anything, to see all the ways in which the existing system is fucked-up, and sometimes it's really hard—or at least harder—to see where the fuckups might lie in the system that might replace it. So it's true, for instance, that open relationships solve the problems of monogamy, but they also create their own set of problems that are just as bad or, in fact, it seems to me, worse.

I really do feel that, in the past thirty years or so, people have gotten a lot better at being in couples. I was talking to a friend of my dad's, I think, who was talking about his son, who's a few years younger than me, who'd recently gotten married, and he was so happy for his kid and so optimistic about his son's relationship. He said, *Yeah, that marriage is really going to last.* He said, *Our generation had no fucking idea what we were doing, but I really think kids today are going into marriage so much better prepared and smarter.* And I really think that's true.

The idea that love is completely magic, and that it's normal and to be expected that you're going to be head over heels in love all the time with the person you're married to, had a lot of currency in the mid-twentieth century. Of course the consequence of that belief is that if you feel something other than this magical emotion, it's a sign of big trouble.

I think that's the typical Hollywood-movie idea of love, which is of course completely toxic and destructive. Then a related idea, probably more of a hippie idea of love, is that the most important thing in a relationship is to be true to yourself, which means that you need to always express everything, and that every emotion you feel has to be addressed, and that the relationship should always make you feel good. This philosophy probably led to a lot of savable marriages of my parents' generation falling apart because people were unwilling to endure the natural difficulty or sacrifice that's part of a desirable marriage.

Speaking of course incredibly generally, I feel that young people today seem to know all this, and I think they go into marriage with an understanding of the kind of communication that's involved and with some sort of realistic idea of what they can expect. And I think the first glimmers of this are starting to happen in child rearing, too. The way people talked about husbands and wives thirty or forty or fifty years ago suggested that love took one of two forms: the ideal Hollywood-movie version of love, where people were just head over heels, no-questions-asked in love with each other, or the "take my wife, please" battle-ax-joke kind of attitude.

I think people are just now starting to bring about that same kind of transformation in their attitudes about child rearing. Up until recently, I think parents described child rearing as this completely wondrous, miraculous thing, in a way that reminds me of the way people used to talk about marriage: something perfect and free of compromise. Or else parents would complain about the kids in an old battle-ax kind of way.

Wouldn't we now be suspicious of someone who talked about their marriage just as a nonstop journey of wonder filled with harp music? Yet people still take that attitude when they talk about their kids. Personally, I'm looking forward to that being less and less the case. Families might be able to work better once people can talk about the experience of child rearing with the same amount of sophistication and nuance we've been able to bring to romantic relationships in the past couple of decades.

28. The Conducting Game

I sometimes do noise games in class settings with smaller groups of ten to twenty people, but I also sometimes do larger participatory events, where an audience of fifty to a hundred people make sounds together for a single performance. For instance, I did a twelve-hour version of a noise event at Nuit Blanche, an overnight arts festival in Toronto, where we brought people in off the street to make sounds together. I did a noise event at a tower in California, and I played noise games with a bunch of programmers at a computer conference.

Here is a music improv game that can be played by a group of ten to a hundred people:

You walk around the room and make sounds, whatever sounds you want. If and when you decide you want to be conducted, you stand still and put your hand up and point at your head.

If you see someone who wants to be conducted, you should conduct them. Don't leave people standing there waiting to be conducted, because it's impolite.

The conducted piece should last about a minute or a minute and a half, and it ends when either person walks away. When you walk away, don't say bye or anything. Just leave. Then you walk around some more.

The notes for conducting are: Conduct with as much specificity as possible in your gestures. Use very clear and deliberate gestures. Be as emphatic as possible. Try to fill each gesture with a lot of urgency and meaning. Trust that the person you're conducting is great at what they do and is going to make great sounds. Know that the gestures will be interpreted as having meanings that you do not intend—that's okay.

For the person being conducted: Trust that the conductor knows exactly what they're doing. Trust that they're a great conductor and that you're excited to work with them. Trust that you know instinctively, immediately, and completely what every single gesture means. Trust that this person is going to extract incredible sounds from you, and that everything that comes out of you—all the sounds that you make—are their responsibility. You should respond to the emotional content in the conducting and ascribe as much meaning as possible to every component of their gestures—their facial expression, whether or not their fingers are curved. Assume that every element of the conducting has meaning.

This game is largely about dialogue and control. It might look like the conductor is in control, but that's not really the case. The game is actually a dialogue between the conductor and the person being conducted. It's a dialogue in which both parties are in a perpetual state of surprise and experiencing lack of control.

For instance, the conductor might slowly raise one fist in the air and then open up all the fingers of his hands and clench his shoulders. No one really knows what that's going to sound like, but the person being conducted very quickly decides what that means and what that sounds like, so both people are being surprised.

As for the person being conducted, if the game is going well, you really feel like the other person is controlling you—you feel *not* in control, like they're making everything happen. But really *you're* the author of all the sounds in the piece. There's not a single sound in it that wasn't devised by you, the person being conducted. It's all choices *you* have made. This is one part of improv that I think is really critical—this experience of feeling not at all responsible while actually being completely responsible.

The same is true for the conductor, but less obviously so.

When you're on the outside watching the game, it's clear that the conductor serves to inspire the sound-maker. If you just put people in a room and say, *I want you to make interesting sounds that change a lot, and that do interesting things and are varied,* people will have a very hard time doing that. But if you put someone in front of them, a person making essentially meaningless gestures, and call that person the conductor and say that the conductor is in charge, then people can make these really amazing sounds. People do fantastic work in this game very quickly. The conductor serves to inspire them, and gives them permission to do much more, by appearing to take away control while not really taking away control.

The conductors can also feel inspired by the people being conducted. If you're asked to make a bunch of really dramatic gestures, you might find that difficult to do, but if you're a conductor in a dialogue with a person who's making these inspiring and incredible sounds, you find you can make really interesting gestures easily and spontaneously. It goes both ways.

29. Sitting on the Same Side of the Table

We're all proud of our society's ability to bring things about without violence. So, for instance, we applaud freely elected governments, where the reins of state can change hands without people having to kill people. But I think that a more advanced version of that goal is to be able to do things without antagonism.

We don't still put people in gladiator rings for amusement. We don't think dueling is an acceptable way for people to settle their differences. But so many of our institutions are still based on models of antagonism as the best way to find solutions to a problem. So in the electoral process you see two candidates running for office, and it always gets presented as a kind of battle. It's true that at some level they're opponents—they both want the office, but there's only one space—but at some level they're also people who want the same thing, to the degree to which they're honest candidates, which I think many people are. What they want is for the country to do well, for people to prosper and be at peace. Even if they do have wildly divergent ideas about how to get there, somehow we've turned the electoral process into a kind of gladiator match where we think the best way to choose a leader is to throw people into a ring and make them fight each other and we can sort of lift up the winner.

It's the same thing with lawmaking institutions. Often, debate is the mode through which legislative ideas are presented. What all the people in that legislative body want—at least in theory—is to produce laws that are fair and serve people well. They may have completely different ideas as to what that constitutes, but there's something that to me feels so atavistic about having people *battle* each other for the right to enter the legislative chamber, then once they're there, to battle each other again to decide what the actual laws should be. It just feels like a throwback to a worse time in humanity.

I'd love to see institutions that somehow operate on the assumption that people can hold vastly different opinions and preferences and desires without having to become enemies, and also without having to lose track of the desires they have that *are* shared.

There's a great book about all this called *Getting to Yes*. It's from the early eighties. In *Getting to Yes*, the authors explain that in a negotiation it helps to literally sit on the same side of the table as each other. And it's hard. It's hard not to keep falling back into the traps of antagonism. So, for instance, if the other side does something that you feel is dishonest or disrespectful, it's hard not to think, *Well, fuck 'em*—even if that *fuck 'em* might mean creating a situation where it's worse for them but also worse for you. This kind of battle approach is hardwired, but it leads to all kinds of lose-lose situations.

The basic idea is to transform a negotiation from a situation where two people are pushing against each other to a situation where people are working toward a common solution. So you may have a lot of different desires and interests and senses of what's fair, but you're also trying to solve a problem together. You want to come to a solution that resolves all those things. And the fact that you want different things doesn't have to make you enemies.

I started thinking about this a lot during my work with the Residents' Association. At the end of it all, the thing that most struck me is how easy it is to get caught up in a battle mentality. You can get so swept up by the idea of winning that you end up forgetting what it is that you're after and focusing instead on stopping your opponent from getting what they want. Just because someone is your opponent doesn't mean that their defeat is always your victory. It's so easy to fall into the trap of thinking that way, but at that point you're no longer acting even to your own advantage. You're just being angry in ways that don't make things better for anybody.

I think a lot of human progress consists of overcoming certain instincts, and understanding that just because someone wants something different from you, it doesn't mean that they're bad or that causing them harm is morally acceptable. But more important, in most cases it also doesn't mean that you'll be better off by hurting them. It's so, so easy to mistake damage to your enemy as a personal gain. This happens on every level: among friends, at work, and in politics.

I know that in law there's a small glimmer of this. Lawyers are now practicing what is known as collaborative divorce. So, where the old model for a divorce settlement was that each party would hire a lawyer and the lawyers would do battle, the collaborative divorce model is that the lawyers and the parties try to work together to come up with what feels like a fair solution to dividing assets and child care and all that, with the understanding that it doesn't make things better for anybody to go to war.

30. Seeing My Friends Drunk
for the First Time

People involved in certain kinds of music and entertainment and culture—what they're really in is the drinks business, since so much of that stuff happens in bars. So Trampoline Hall is in the drinks business. There's more money in bar sales than in ticket sales, and that affects how a lot of these events are structured.

When I first started my games night, something I thought was, *So many of the things that happen in bars are such boring experiences*, and I figured a games night would be a way to give people a more engaging experience in bars. I thought, *People go to bars because they want to be around other people*, but normally being in bars doesn't give you much opportunity to interact with other people, and I thought the games nights would sort of solve that problem.

What I didn't understand at the time was that a lot of things I viewed as problems were actually part of the business model. So in Toronto, at least, when you go to see a band, it usually starts later than it's scheduled to, and there's more time between the sets than you feel you need, and it's boring. But all that boredom sells drinks. If you make people stand around in a bar for half an hour with nothing to do, eventually they'll buy a drink if for no other reason than that it kills five minutes to buy the drink and then it gives them something to do with their hands afterward.

At the games night, people were pretty much fully engaged and entertained from the moment they got there till the moment they left, so they didn't end up buying all the drinks that normally get bought out of boredom, so the bar never made any money. If the bar doesn't make any money, the business that you're in isn't really functioning. I thought that barroom events were in the business of entertaining people, and they are, but sort of in the same way that television for the first few decades of its existence wasn't really in the business of entertaining people, it was in the business of entertaining people just enough that they could be persuaded to watch the ads, which is where the actual money came from. In the same way, all the entertainment that's in a bar is primarily there just to get you to buy drinks, and if it fails to get you to buy drinks, you're not really doing your job as the organizer of the event.

I'm always a little bit baffled by bars where there's no dancing but the music is incredibly loud, and I don't really understand why people would want to hang around and mingle in a place where it's impossible to be heard. I suspect that one reason for that, again, is that it sells more drinks; if it's easier to have a conversation, there's less need for the activity of going back and forth to the bar. I don't know.

Drinking isn't a big part of the events I run now, and at some events it's discouraged if not completely forbidden. Partly, in the beginning, I was interested in how the participatory improvisation stuff might be an alternative to drinking and drugs—a way to have a raucous party where the energy came from something other than intoxicants. At that time in my life, I did go to a lot of parties and I always wanted something wild and exciting and unusual to happen, but mostly people would just sort of get drunk, and nothing exciting and wild and amusing would happen. To me, there was a real contrast between that and getting people together for theater games or even charades, where people end up doing things that really *are* surprising. Someone might be crawling around on the floor pretending to be a dog while other people point and shout at them, or a hundred people might be getting swept up in a sort of transcendent aesthetic experience while chasing each other around a room. These all seemed to me, at the time, like the kinds of things that drugs and parties should produce but that drugs and parties mostly didn't.

When I first started doing charades parties, as this sort of house party/art project with a friend of mine, we played multiple parlor games in different rooms, and I found that once people had a few drinks, they couldn't really play the games anymore.

I think it was the first time in my life I'd ever really seen drunk people. I'd always been one of them before. When you're drunk and all your friends are drunk, you think you're all really charming and funny, but at those parties I sort of thought, *Well, I'm at work*—so I didn't drink. But all my amusing friends did, and seeing them from the perspective of sobriety was kind of awful. It's not that you become more interesting and fun when you're drunk, it's that your perception of interesting and fun is lowered to such a moronic level. And mostly people become bad. The teams fight more with each other, people don't pay attention. With lots of the stuff I do, I think people can't do it when they're drunk, and I'm less interested in it if they are.

I used to drink a lot and do drugs the normal amount, because it made things more fun. In the end, I decided that if these things lead you into genuinely fun, interesting places, that's okay, but if they lead you to places that wouldn't be fun if you weren't drunk, it's a little bit depressing. That's one of the many reasons why drinking isn't as bad for young people as it is for older people. When people are nineteen, they get drunk and it really *does* lead them into interesting misadventure, or they wind up in a new part of town—and that's what you *want* when you're nineteen. The drugs and alcohol help make that more possible in a number of ways. When you're older, drugs and alcohol just give you greater tolerance for a boring time.

31. A Decision Is a Thing You Make

A couple of years ago, I got to the point where I felt I had no idea what I was doing. I mean, I was doing many projects and a lot of them were really interesting and fun, and sort of well received in the small world in which I operate, but I wasn't making any money. Also, I had no idea what it all added up to. At first I thought I just needed to figure out how to make money and keep doing what I was doing, but then I came to the conclusion that I didn't really know where I was trying to get to in my life, and in my working life especially. If someone had said, *Where do you want your working life to be in five years?* I would have had no way of answering that question. Somehow my life had got filled up with weird experiments and side projects, but there wasn't anything at the core of it.

I think it happened like this: In the mid-nineties, I had a job in Toronto doing Internet stuff, and I got fired from that job after trying to unionize my office, so I ended up doing freelance web development at a time when that was a tremendously lucrative thing to do. Around that time, I was also really attached to the idea of leisure, so I worked only a few days a week. I made a lot of money, I had a lot of free time, and I really wanted to fill it intelligently with things that were fun. Those "fun" projects eventually started to take over my life, and after a couple of years, it seemed I was working seventy hours a week, not making any money, doing things that were "fun."

Teaching classes in how to play charades isn't the most practical idea in the world, and neither is running a lecture series featuring nonexperts, and neither is teaching theater classes but refusing to admit actors.

How could any of these things make any money or lead anywhere? This worried me a lot and it was a terrible time for me in a lot of ways. After a couple of years I sort of felt like, well, I need some results. You can't just experiment forever. You have to *act* on it—act on the data that you've gathered, or something. I felt upset at myself. I felt that I'd been foolish to imagine that somehow the answer to how I would live and work and make money would present itself if I ran around long enough doing different things.

I decided to go to the bookstore and look at some self-help books about careers. I went and found two or three books that looked pretty good. I took them home and I read them. It was pretty exciting.

I'm a real believer in certain kinds of self-help books. A lot of them, of course, are really, really terrible—like anything—but when they're good I think they're great. It's easy to underestimate the fact that other people have had similar problems to yours and that you can learn from their experiences—and learn from people who've spent lots of time thinking about certain problems. A well-written self-help book can stop you from going down all kinds of blind alleys and trying all sorts of solutions that happen not to work.

One of these books was written by a guy who ran a consulting business, and you could hire him or his folks to help you out. That seemed pretty good to me, because I liked the book quite a bit. So I called him up and I was able to work with him. The deal was that you work over the phone, and he gives you assignments, and then you do the assignments and call him back.

What made me like his book was a section called "How to Make Decisions," which is something that I—at that time in my life—was terrible at. And I was upset at myself for being so terrible at it.

Basically, the chapter explained in some detail the kinds of factors that go into making a decision. It explained that first you needed to figure out what you wanted—what your priorities were—which was a process that he didn't make out to be terribly mysterious or anything, but he pointed out that it took some time and some thinking. Then you have to collect information from the world to try to get a sense of what your options are and what likely outcomes of different courses of action are. Then he tells you how to write these things up—maybe put them in a chart. At the end of the section, what he said was: *Now once you've done all this, make the decision.*

And I really liked that! Basically the point of the section was you can't externalize the project of making a decision. You can't hope there's going to be an algorithm to make the decision for you which will perfectly rationalize it. You can be better about it and try to be better informed, but there's no getting around the fact that you have to make a decision. That's how a decision happens.

That's a really important thing that sometimes nervous people like me don't realize—that the expression "to make a decision" is perfectly accurate: a decision is something you *create*. There's an inclination to think that with enough research and thinking and conversation and information, it's possible to determine what the *correct* decision is; to think that decision making is an intellectual puzzle. But generally it's not. You *make* decisions. Something is created when you make a decision. It's an act of will, not an act of thought.

So I was very excited to do all this. I talked to the guy who wrote the book, and I decided to go ahead with this project. I worked on it for a while. I talked to him on the phone. I made lists. I had meetings with my friends—which was my favorite part. I interviewed my friends and I asked them not so much for advice about what I should do but what they thought I was interested in and what they thought I was good at and what they thought I wasn't good at. Sometimes that would lead specifically to ideas for careers and sometimes it wouldn't. The idea was to do some data gathering about myself and my proclivities, and it was a real pleasure.

Generally, my friends thought I liked new things and got bored with things easily. Almost everybody in some way or another mentioned that they couldn't really see me having a job where I did the same thing all the time, which is funny, because I'm someone who thinks of myself as liking routine. It was interesting to realize the degree to which I work and think well with other people in real time, and to understand that that's not true of everybody. For me it only seems natural, of course. How can you come up with good ideas except in dialogue with someone else, or onstage, or in a situation like that? But I realized that for a lot of people that's not true at all. One reason people are, for instance, well suited to being writers is that they have a strong ability, or in many cases a preference, to do their thinking alone. People talked about my ability to think on my feet. Teaching was something that came up a lot. It was interesting, too, that some people felt that I already had a career—that what I was doing was already sort of coherent and clear to them, even if it wasn't to me.

After a while, having worked on more exercises and having done more research, I realized I had to make a decision. But it became harder and harder to get my thoughts together. I would sit down every day to try to refine my plan, and I would just be overwhelmed with terror. I'd be completely paralyzed. I imagine this is what people must feel like when they have a dissertation that they never finish or another big project that they never finish. In this case the big project was figuring out what I should do with my life. I woke up every morning thinking, *I'm terribly far behind on the project of my whole life.*

I think there was a point at which I finally wrote up a page description of a working life that I gave to this guy, and we talked on the phone, and he was like, *That's it—that's what you want to do. Now it's your job to figure out how to do that.*

The basic idea was a mix of teaching classes in impractical

subjects with more practical applications of similar kinds of work, like doing training or conferences or those kinds of things. So when he was like, *Yeah, you've got it*, I think for about five minutes I felt really good. But then I felt bad. I was really frightened about whether this actually was the right choice. I was frightened about all the other possibilities this ruled out, which is kind of the *definition* of choice. It was great to have his encouragement, but it sort of felt to me like he'd made the decision himself, and I wasn't sure if I completely trusted him.

I ended up seeing a therapist who was interested in professional stuff but was also a psychologist, and he had a very different take on these issues. What I learned from him was that when you're in a situation of uncertainty that's causing you pain, as I was in my life, there's a couple of things you can do.

One thing you can do is increase your certainty, and the other thing you can do is increase your tolerance for uncertainty. The stuff that I was doing with this guy was, in my mind at least, based on the idea that my goal was to completely eliminate uncertainty—that the task ahead of me was to figure out the perfect job for myself, the perfect career, and that I would then make this very difficult decision, and once that was behind me I wouldn't have to face this painful uncertainty anymore.

I think there's a lot to be said for making decisions and for making choices and for introducing certainty. But there's no way you're going to eliminate uncertainty.

I think realizing that was really important for me.

32. All the Games Are Meant to Solve Problems, but Problems Are Unpleasant

A lot of my games come from things that go wrong in my classes. I have a class and I have some expectation of how I want people to respond to some exercise, but they don't respond the way I want them to, or they're too shy, or they don't believe that the sounds they're making are musical, or there's too much variation in comfort among the different participants in the class, or they're always making the same kinds of sounds and won't do anything different. Whenever I have a problem like this, I usually get upset, and then I have to invent a game to fix it. Usually it works, and then I'm happy. But it always seems dumb that I get upset. I wish I could somehow learn this lesson: that one of the main reasons I teach the classes is to generate new games—and that that's one of the greatest pleasures. By far the most productive source of new games is new problems. So you'd think I'd be happy when new problems present themselves, but I never am.

33. Home Maladies

Every once in a while, whenever we're cleaning up the house, Margaux is like, *How come you have seven copies of* The Doctors Book of Home Remedies? *Please could you throw out six of the copies?* And I always say, *Sweetheart, no, I use them for a game. They're for my class. I need them all.*

This game is about wholeheartedly accepting what other people give you to deal with in a theater scene. There's a classic theater exercise where people give each other gifts, and each person is meant to give and accept gifts as warmly as possible. The *Home Remedies* game is just the same stupid game, except we use that book. Player one comes onstage and she says to player two, *Oh, I got you a gift*—and hands player two *The Doctors Book of Home Remedies*. And player two says, *Oh, that's so kind of you! You got me*—and then he opens the book at a random page and chooses the malady that's at the top of the page. You know, *You got me diarrhea*. At which point he is inflicted with the most severe case of whatever that malady is, while also expressing much joy and gratitude for the generous gift. Then the process is reversed. He says to player one, *Oh, that reminds me, I got you something*—and back and forth they go, happily contracting a variety of diseases. It's a completely moronic game, but it gets people accustomed to the idea that they don't have to run away from bad things in scenes, and it plays with the tension between delight and horribleness that I think makes up a lot of the fun of improv.

The Doctors Book of Home Remedies is a pretty good

source for ailments, by the way, partly because there's roughly one per page, but also because there tends not to be home remedies for really serious sicknesses, so people aren't constantly giving each other leukemia, which might be less funny. They're more likely to be giving each other dandruff or stuttering.

34. Keeping Away People Who
Would Be Disappointed

The people I might want to attend my classes are exactly those people who might feel nervous about attending my classes. This makes it hard to figure out how to discourage the people who I suspect really *will* hate the classes. I give out questionnaires beforehand, and I ask things like, *Are you okay being in a situation where you're going to make and listen to a lot of discordant sounds?* I also ask people what they expect they'll get out of the class, and every once in a while someone might write that they're trying to become a more proficient jazz improviser, or that they're an improv comedian who wants to get better at making up funny songs. Usually I phone these people and I say, *Um, I notice you said you were interested in this—and I want to make sure that this class will provide what you're looking for*. I might point them to one of the videos on YouTube of fifteen people screaming in a room. I usually don't hear from these people again.

35. The Happiness Class

I taught a class on happiness to my friends, and one thing that came up was that the topic was seen as sort of trivial. I found that really weird. It was seen as some sort of sickness of Western consumerist individualism. Happiness seems to me the *most* un-trivial thing to talk about or think about. I think it's really worthy of investigation. Pretty much everything that people do, in one way or another, is done in the interest of trying to be happy. So it doesn't seem like a bad idea to spend a bit of one's time thinking about it.

You can say, for instance, that environmental damage is a more important issue than happiness, but a huge part of what drives environmental damage is people's weird consumerist appetites for goods, acquired in the pursuit of happiness, which don't actually make their lives any happier. Most of history is about people killing each other for things they imagine they want and things they imagine are going to make them happier, which in most cases aren't the sorts of things that make people happier at all.

I find it interesting that people spend their whole lives aggressively pursuing things, at great cost, that they *imagine* will make them happy, when in fact these things don't. And I think this is a problem for many people.

In the past few years, there has been a lot of research into happiness, and along with that, a lot of press, and a lot of books taking that research and trying to apply it to people's lives. A couple of years ago, I discovered that there was an undergraduate course at Harvard which had quickly become the most popular under-graduate course in the history of the university. It was a course in how to be happy. I was really delighted by this. I thought it was a great idea, and I was sorry they didn't have that class when I was there, and I was very excited to know more about it.

I invited a dozen friends to my house so that we could take it together. The course, famously a comically easy course at Harvard, still involved several hours' reading a week. So I took on the task of presenting a condensed version of the course to my friends, which involved me watching all the videos and choosing select moments to show and trying to select the most useful readings.

Every week for a couple of months, we would get together in me and Margaux's kitchen, which is also our bedroom, and I would set up my laptop and bring in the screen from my desk and set it up on the kitchen table, and we would watch this guy, Professor Tal Ben-Shahar, lecture to something like seven hundred Harvard undergraduates on how to be happy. Then we would talk about it, and I would ask if anybody had done the reading, and no one had ever done the reading. It was great.

I thought the material in the course was really interesting, and I also really wanted to alter my own immediate social environment. I had all these people around me who were really interesting and kind of eccentric and sort of crazy, and I wanted to establish a common language about what the hell we thought we were trying to do in our lives, and I imagined this would be a good way to do it. And it was. It was really exciting to get people talking about what they were trying to do in their lives and their work, about why or whether they thought this might contribute to their happiness, and to expose the differences that were there, and just to find out what people thought they were up to. It's funny: you can talk to people for a very, *very* long time about what they're doing without ever finding out what they think they're up to.

·

Among everybody in the class, there was incredible disagreement about the relationship between difficulty and happiness and work and where pleasure comes from, and the conversations about this were really heated and contentious.

For Margaux, difficulty is everything. She's an artist and she thinks that making art is really hard and should be hard. Not to say that there isn't a great amount of pleasure in it, but part of what it means to do that work is to encounter the difficulty in it. She always seems to be working. When she does stop working, she tidies the house. When she watches TV, she makes a quilt. It's very hard for her to understand sightseeing if there's no effort involved. So driving up to the top of a mountain to look at a beautiful view seems to her a completely useless activity, whereas walking up a mountain to look at a view is something that really excites her. This is the reason we have a lot of fights when we go to mountains.

Almost diametrically opposed is my friend Edward. One of the complicated things in his life is that when he was younger he was in bands. A lot of the people around him are artists and writers and things like that, and he thinks of himself as a creative person and sort of has this fantasy of being an artist, and he maybe feels bad not to be doing that kind of work. He's a really smart guy and my impression is that he's super-good at his job designing databases, and he seems to like it. But there's this part of him that feels he should be doing something more creative. I think he imagines that there's an emotional place he can be, where he's inspired to make art and does it because it comes naturally and it's fun and exciting. I think Edward believes mostly in hedonism. He mostly believes that the trick to life is to do things that are easy and fun, and that it's possible to avoid things that are difficult. And he's frustrated when that doesn't seem to work out. He imagines if things were just a little different, he'd have this easy, inspired, creative life. Yet making art *is* difficult for people who do that kind of work.

My friend Mark is working on a book. He wants working on the book to be something fun in his life, so he only works on it when he feels like it, and when he doesn't feel like it, he doesn't. Margaux finds this completely outrageous! She thinks you can't make art by working on it when you feel like it. You have to work on it when you *don't* feel like it, partly because otherwise it will never get done, but more important because those times when you don't feel like it—when you encounter resistance or difficulty— are the times when the really important work happens. She thinks that difficulty is an indication that you're going somewhere new or challenging.

Darren O'Donnell, a theater artist we know, thinks that all the difficulty in his life can be traced back to an unjust society. He thinks he'd be much happier if he could spend all of his time at leisure, but capitalism means he can't, partly because he needs to make money and partly because he feels morally obliged to address an unjust system through his art. His feeling about having to work and having to encounter difficulty in his work is primarily one of resentment, and he spends a lot of time thinking, *If only things weren't like this.*

An idea I've come across a lot in my reading about happiness is that maybe we're not really designed to be happy—from an evolutionary standpoint. Maybe happiness is, at best, a temporary state that functions as an incentive to the behaviors that biology wants from us, and that we're meant to strive for.

So we strive and we strive. And a lot of the striving on the face of it can seem meaningless or dumb. Mark sees people around him who work hard so they can have a nice apartment and nice stuff, and Mark thinks that's silly; why not just have a small crappy apartment and not much stuff and not have to do all that hard work?

And it's true: we get caught up striving for things that can seem really important at the time but which don't actually help us at all. If you step back, it's easy to see that a lot of this striving is meaningless or pointless. At the same time, to imagine that we could be happy without all this effort is unrealistic. It's to imagine us as something other than what we are. I think we're always meant to do *some* meaningless striving, or at least that we're not happy without it. It's a bit of a cosmic joke, I think, but I do think it's the way we're built.

You'd think that a good way to be happy would be to maximize the number of things in your life that are pleasurable and easy, and to minimize the number of things in your life that are unpleasurable and difficult. But my own experience doesn't seem to bear that out, and neither does the research on the subject. A confusing thing about happiness is that hedonism happens not to work. At least not for most people. Certainly not for me.

So Darren really believes that he would be happy if only the wickedness of society didn't require him, in all these different ways, to continue to work. You work and work and work, then you get to spend ten minutes lying on the grass, and lying on the grass feels wonderful. And it's easy to think, *Man, if only those fuckers didn't make me work all the time, I could spend all my time lying on the grass and I'd feel good.* But it wouldn't feel good to lie on the grass all the time.

I mean, even Buddhist monks, who are sort of the counterexample to all that—they say that maybe you *can* be happy sitting in one spot, breathing in and breathing out, accepting everything as it is—and it's a strong point they make, and a pretty shocking one, too, to suggest that maybe the path to happiness is to give up pretty much *everything*, to not really do anything at all—but even within that, those monks, with their adherence to not striving, they work really *hard* on that, you know?

36. The Converge / Diverge Game

This is a game and also a music piece. Here's how it works:

The first step is to ask people to make whatever sounds they want, so the result is a cacophony of everyone making different sounds. Then you instruct people to converge gradually—to come to a point where they are making the same sound. They make that same sound for a while, then gradually diverge from that point until eventually they are making sounds that are very different from each other again. Then you repeat. That's basically how it works.

You want the convergence to feel like something that just happens. There shouldn't be a bunch of hand-waving and signaling; there should just be listening. Most important, it shouldn't be something where one person dominates and everyone joins that person's sound. To someone listening to the game, it should sound gradual. A good strategy for players is to start incorporating other people's sounds into their own, gradually, as they move toward convergence. There's a strong inclination when people are moving toward a sound to get the details rounded off things, but good players will learn how not to do that. If there are small details over which there is disagreement, players should err on the side of more and sharper detail, paying special attention to things like timbre and emotion. They shouldn't let those disappear. They should exaggerate them, if necessary.

When they're at the point where they have converged and are making the same sound, they should take time to really get the unison as accurate as they possibly can and to listen for points of disagreement and to sharpen details so the unison is really close to perfect. Let the players continue to make this same sound together for a while. People can enjoy this for a lot longer than you might expect. There's a pretty deep pleasure in that unison, in making the same sound over and over, especially when it took some work to get there.

Then, when the players start moving apart or diverging, the main challenge is that the divergence should sound very gradual to a listener. If everyone in the group simultaneously makes a small change, it will sound to the listener like an enormous change, so people should start diverging at different times. As an individual player, one way to make the divergence sound gradual is not to diverge at all. As the divergence intensifies, a challenge to the players is to think about different ways to keep components of the converged sound even while moving further out. Finally, for a while, the players can just make their own sounds and listen to each other as they would in a regular improvisation, but before beginning to reconverge they should try to move to a point of even greater divergence than they're currently at, and the way to do that is for each player to listen to what is going on in the room and try to do the thing that is most opposite to what they hear.

On one level, it's a very simple exercise in how you can have tension and resolution in a piece of music without pitch. The resolution is unison and the tension is chaos.

It also makes you think about how a group can make a collective decision, inching toward it gradually, without a leader, and with most opportunities for communication removed.

This game really also ties in with ideas about mistakes and their beauty, sometimes. One thing that makes it interesting to listen to as a piece of music can be the way players are failing at it as a game. It's interesting to hear sounds converge toward each other, but if everyone did it perfectly it wouldn't be as interesting to listen to. So the sounds of people who in the game are failing or getting it wrong, in the musical piece might be the sounds that are the most interesting and pretty. What are the mistakes from one perspective are the successes from another.

37. Going to Parties

I remember having this conversation with someone a while ago, and he wanted to start having regular parties, and he was really vehement about this one point: he was like, *These parties aren't going to be work-networking parties.* He said, *You go to parties and people are trying to form professional connections, or they're trying to pick people up, or they're trying to get some other thing done.* He said, *Why do parties always have to be like that? My parties are going to be different.*

And I found that absolutely baffling. People want to *get* things out of parties—that's important to remember. Anyone who tells you they're going to a party for no reason, or anyone who tells you they're throwing parties but don't want the attendees to feel like they're trying to get something out of them, is lying, kidding themselves, or dumb.

Sometimes people want sex. Sometimes people want to get drunk or take drugs. Some people enjoy dancing. Some people are trying to meet new people to make their life better in some way—because they want new friends or new opportunities in their work. Some people want opportunities to behave inappropriately or get into fights.

If you find you don't want anything from parties anymore, you should probably stop going. You won't have any fun.

Here is some other advice about parties:

At cocktail parties, you don't have to talk as much as you might think. No one cares if you're not talking. You might feel very awkward, but no one really minds. Especially if you want to be thought clever, you don't have to talk a lot. Just say one or two smart things.

If you're actually in a conversation, you can listen. People always appreciate that.

If you're standing there not doing anything, you probably feel tremendously awkward, but no one cares. No one's paying any attention to you. Unfortunately, once you realize this, it takes away a lot of what energizes a party. I think a lot of what energizes a cocktail party is people's fear of being seen not talking to anyone.

Also, the last six hours of a party usually aren't much fun.

Parties *should* be fun. They should be gone to out of a desire to get something out of them. Certainly you shouldn't go out of obligation to the host. It's bad for the party. If you want to express affection for someone, maybe there are ways to do that that are less draining of your soul than going to their party.

38. Kensington Market

There's a neighborhood in Toronto called Kensington Market, which is my favorite neighborhood in Toronto and probably one of my favorite neighborhoods in the world. It's a really remarkable place. I lived there for six or seven years when I first moved to Toronto, till I was illegally evicted so that a new landlord could charge a higher rent, which is kind of important in terms of my feelings about the place.

Traditionally, the neighborhood has been an immigrant neighborhood. It's gone through a lot of stages of different immigrant groups being there over the decades, and all those different groups are sort of layered up in the Market, so there's evidence of the Jewish population that lived there early in the century, which was followed by the Portuguese and Vietnamese and Caribbean, and also for a long time it's been a place where a certain number of artists and young people and writers and musicians have lived. It's really a distinct place in Toronto: little streets and shops— butchers, fruit stands, and that kind of thing. It's one of the few neighborhoods in Toronto that is not just a long street. Kensington Market is actually a little winding grid of tiny one-way streets.

A few years ago, some people thought it would be a good idea to improve Kensington by getting rid of cars. As a first step, they worked with the City to organize a series of Pedestrian Sundays, which were large, car-free street festivals every Sunday of the summer.

I was out one day and I ran into the first one of these. And it just felt awful to me. The neighborhood on a regular Sunday is a really great and remarkable place. The festival replaced that.

It seemed to me at the time that there are a million things wrong with the idea of pedestrianizing the Market. One problem is that it's simplistic, in that it fails to understand that different things are interconnected in a city. People imagine that if they took the cars out of Kensington Market, what they would be left with is Kensington Market as it is now, but just with no cars. But that's wrong. A neighborhood is like an ecosystem. If you take out one component, especially a component as important and influential as cars, it changes things completely. Like with an ecosystem, it's very, very hard to predict what actually will happen, but you can take some pretty good guesses here.

Some businesses really depend on cars. In Kensington, those businesses are places like the butchers that sell large orders to restaurants and to immigrant families who now live in the suburbs but still come to the old neighborhood to do their shopping—and stores that sell fruits and spices which do a lot of deliveries and moving of goods in and out. These are the stores that are the traditional backbone of the neighborhood.

Then there are stores that don't rely as much on cars and that rely more on pedestrian traffic, along with businesses which are entertainment destinations: cafés, bistros, shops that cater to tourists who come to walk around, used-clothing stores.

In terms of the ecosystem of the Market, something one might predict if you eliminate cars is that you'll accelerate a trend which is already happening to some degree, which is that the Market becomes more of an entertainment destination than a functional neighborhood.

There's also a kind of class blindness in this. Some activists talk about cars and bikes as if cyclists and pedestrians are the oppressed underdogs. But in a lot of ways, the ability to get around the city by foot and bike represents something of a position of privilege. It means you live close to downtown, and you don't have a crappy job that you have to commute to. So the reality of who actually cycles in the city is that it tends to be a somewhat privileged class of able-bodied people who can afford to live a certain kind of life in a dense downtown core. That's great, but to make motorists into the enemy, you have to understand that in a lot of cases you're talking about working-class people who don't get to live downtown, who have families to support. It's not like Kensington Market is full of sports cars and Mercedeses.

So while they may not have realized it, what it seemed to me the pedestrian activists were really advocating was taking the most interesting, organic neighborhood in the whole city and turning it into an entertainment destination.

I would say, *There's a real chance you'll turn this into a tourist destination*, and some people would say, *No—it'll always be Kensington*. They'd say, *It's not like it's going to turn into Yorkville*. Because it's unimaginable to them that a neighborhood like Kensington could turn into a neighborhood like Yorkville— which is the most upscale neighborhood in Toronto—yet Yorkville *was* a neighborhood like Kensington not long ago! People sometimes have a really hard time imagining these transformations.

Neighborhoods that are really good, I think, are places that feel like people live there. When you throw a huge, noisy street party every Sunday, it really creates the impression that people *don't* live there, because who in the world would choose to have this outside their window? Who would think that what their own neighborhood needs is to have a drum circle and an amplified performance poet outside their own home every single Sunday all summer? So a festival like that creates the message that the neighborhood belongs to the people who come there as an entertainment destination, not to the people who live there.

I started talking to people to do research for an article I wanted to write about this. It was the first and only time in my adult life that I felt like I wanted to write an editorial for the newspaper. There had been lots of press about people who supported the project but hardly any about people who objected, and it turned out that there was a lot of objection. Many businesses were opposed because they felt it would be very damaging to their business not to have access by car. Lots of neighbors were opposed because they found it disruptive and noisy and it took away what they loved about Kensington Market. On Sunday afternoons in the summer, Kensington as a neighborhood was no longer accessible to them.

In terms of the shopkeepers, some of them didn't speak English. A lot of them were from places where individual input into public decision isn't exactly encouraged—where you can get into trouble for speaking your mind about things and dissenting. So it was pretty easy for them to feel like they couldn't protest or that their opinions would be overlooked in favor of the opinions of a bunch of enthusiastic, educated young environmentalists.

My position was that Kensington Market is an area worth preserving. There's an argument against my position, which is a fair argument, which is to say that neighborhoods change, it's silly to try to preserve things, and you don't want to turn Kensington into a museum of itself. I think that's a coherent position. But what's not a coherent position is to imagine that you can make Kensington completely pedestrian *without* radically changing it. If you advocate pedestrianization, you have to understand that you're accelerating certain existing trends. You can't pretend you're just *allowing* change to happen—you're pushing things in a specific direction, and, in this case, you need to be honest with yourself about what the likely consequences of that are.

There's also a question of what's fair and what's democratic. In the case of Kensington, the people whose voices were most being ignored were tenants and immigrant shopkeepers. So you have to be careful, I think, and be on the lookout that the change you're proposing is not just for the benefit of the most vocal groups and businesses while being damaging to the people who aren't as easily heard from.

All this was a few years ago, and a lot has changed. Most notably, I think that even among the people who are big fans of Pedestrian Sundays, a lot of them are now of the opinion that fully pedestrianizing the Market would be a bad thing. I think I may have contributed to that shift in opinion, which feels good. My sense is that the event organizers are now doing a good job of getting more members of the neighborhood involved in decision making, including people who initially disliked the event.

In some ways it's sad for me to see the transformation of the neighborhood continue, but I suspect that that is the sort of change you do have to put up with if you don't want to be a crazy person.

39. Keeping People Quiet

At the beginning of every Trampoline Hall show, I give the audience instructions on how best to enjoy the show. I tell them to sit, and to sit as close to the stage as possible. I tell them what the show will entail, so that they don't become antsy. People always think I'm joking when I tell them—from the stage, speaking through the mike—that the show will be starting in three minutes, then two minutes. But I'm not. I tell them how many acts there will be and around how long they will be, and when there will be breaks. Really, all these things are there to make it easier for people in the audience to pay attention; to know what's expected of them and what they can expect. I think it's much easier to pay attention if you know you're going to have to pay attention for half an hour. In a way, it's a kind of contract.

One of the very last things I do when I give people instructions on how to enjoy the show is that I encourage them to shush other people if they are talking. I give them some different techniques for doing this. I tell them if they want to be direct and aggressive, they can turn around and shush the person angrily, or if they prefer a more passive-aggressive style, they can cover their mouths with their hands so no one will know who did the shushing.

When I say all this stuff at the beginning of the show, again, I think people mostly think I'm joking, but inevitably during any show in a bar, people eventually do talk, and instead of me having to reprimand them from the stage in some authoritarian way, when someone talks a number of people in the audience do the shushing. Then the people talking understand that the desire for quiet during the show is a collective desire, and they tend to stop talking. As a performer on the stage, this saves you the terrible indignity of having to ask the audience every five minutes to simmer down and listen to you.

40. Feeling Like a Fraud

The feeling I have before taking on any interesting project, especially teaching classes, is pretty much a feeling of terror and sickness. I think that's really not evident to people involved in my projects, because so much of what the projects are about is taking crazy risks and doing ridiculous things and, on the surface, not caring so much about outcomes. But maybe in part because of all that, I have such a fear that these projects will be bad or that they're terrible ideas or that I'm being a fraud in some way.

So before every series, and sometimes before every class, the main thing that often goes through my head is, *I have nothing to offer these people—they will realize that I am a fraud—I have nothing to say about this.*

I think it's worthwhile for people to know that. I think a lot of art is about creating the illusion of ease, and I think it's great to enjoy that illusion, but I think it's great to know that it's an illusion, and I suspect—in my experience—the process of creating anything involves quite a lot of fear and difficulty, and it also involves covering up quite a lot of that fear and difficulty.

So, for example, you get an email from me announcing that I'm teaching a class in how to play charades, and you think, *What a crazy idea, and what a delightful happy-go-lucky person who's doing something as impractical as teaching a class in charades.* But in fact I'm waking up in the middle of the night having panic attacks. About a fucking charades class.

I don't know. I just think it's important for people to know these things.

41. Negotiation

That final Residents' Association meeting with the city councillor really stuck with me a long time. I thought often about how
amazing it was to find common interest among people who
seemed like they were at war with one another. A while later, I
was really excited when I discovered that there was a whole area
of study around this. I started to read a lot of smart, good books
about negotiation that captured my imagination in a way in
which almost nothing else had. I also started reading in related
fields in the social sciences—looking into game theory and subjects like that—and I started working with people who taught
negotiation classes, which I found really amazing. The field is
such a tremendous combination of intellectual, analytical
problem-solving skills, mixed in with very personal stuff about
people's feelings.

I remember hearing a talk about the environment given by,
I think it was Justin Trudeau, the son of Pierre Trudeau. He said
the only issue anyone should be working on is the environment.
He said, *You might disagree with me. You might have some
other issue that you think is more important, like hunger, but
whatever issue it is, if we don't solve the problem of global warm-
ing, your other issue doesn't matter, because everyone's going to
be destroyed.*

From my point of view, you're not going to solve the problem of the environment without getting to a better understanding of how people can cooperate with each other. No matter
how much science you do on atmospheric changes and weather
patterns, the fact is that any solution will require a combined

worldwide effort between a huge number of individuals, and governments, and corporations. And that cooperation—that's where the biggest challenge lies. It's true for climate change and it's true for most of the huge issues facing the world. So the most important thing is figuring out how people can get better at coming to agreement.

42. Fighting Games

A lot of the games I do involve fighting. When I do a theater class, about half of it is fighting. When I do a music class, about half of it is fighting. Some people really take to the fighting and like it, and some people are a little bit offended or upset by it. But I think pretend fighting is a fundamental component of what play is. When you look at play behavior in young animals, a lot of what they do when they play is pretend to fight. And a game is a pretend competition, or a pretend battle between people.

So when people say, *Why aren't your games more positive?* I think it's funny, because niceness doesn't have to happen in a game. You should be nice in real life. You don't have to *play* at niceness. You can just do it. Fighting is something to be minimized in real life. A good way to know that you're playing is if you're doing something you would never do in real life—like having a ridiculous fight.

I have a series of fighting games where I have people pair up and have them do arguments in gibberish, using language-like sounds but no actual language. I teach a series of forms or styles of fighting, kind of like a martial art for ridiculous arguments.

FORM 1

In form 1, there's only one person "speaking" at one time: there are no pauses, and there are never two people speaking at once. You absolutely *must* speak until someone interrupts you, and when the other person interrupts you, you absolutely must stop.

You can interrupt them right back a microsecond later, but you have to let them interrupt you.

FORM 2

Like in form 1, there's always exactly only one person speaking at once, but the difference here is that you may *never* interrupt the other person. Instead, when the other person stops, you *must* start speaking.

FORM 3

In form 3, both people speak at the same time, all the time. No one ever stops. A challenge in this form—though it's one that comes pretty naturally to people—is to be able to speak and listen at once, to respond even though you're never actually stopping to listen.

FORM 4

At any given moment, either both people are speaking, as in form 3, or both people are silent. However, in the moments when both people are silent, they must both be in motion. During the silence, the argument continues, but wordlessly. The fighters circle each other around the room and make gestures and so on.

FORM 5

Here, both players are silent all the time and are always in motion.

Usually after I teach these five forms, I'll introduce a sixth form, called "freestyle," which is to say that after learning all these forms, students are allowed to invoke any of the forms and do whatever they want at any time. It can seem like a joke—like I've taught all these rules just to take them away—but it's not a joke, and the rules aren't really taken away. What I genuinely want is for people to feel free to do what they want to do within this range of options, but to be really aware of what they're doing.

I'm very interested in the combination of abandon and structure in improvisation, and fighting games combine tremendous abandon with a very tight structure. People are typically very good at losing themselves in fighting games, because anger is a pretty easy emotion to tap into, and because people are not being asked to come up with words or a story.

VARIATION 1

I'll sometimes introduce the concept of winners and losers into freestyle arguments. Instead of lasting forever, each argument has an ending. One possible ending is this: at any given moment, one of the players must start to cry and collapse onto the floor, at which point the other player must do a victory dance.

People have very different responses to this variation. Some people have trouble making themselves the crier. Some people have trouble doing the victory dance. But usually people get over these difficulties pretty quickly.

VARIATION 2

In this variation, the battle for victory becomes more intense. At any moment in the fight, one of the players can raise their hands and cower, as if being physically threatened by the other player. This means that the other player now has a weapon. As the cowering player backs up, the other player has to threaten them. Then the player with the weapon can throw their hands up, thereby indicating that the other player has a bigger weapon, and the roles reverse. This exchange can go back and forth as long as the players like. At any given moment, the player being threatened can choose to end the arms race by refusing to cower, and by yelling back instead, at which point the fight reverts to normal arguing.

What I like about these variations is that the power in the exercise is put into the hands of the person who's powerless in the story. So you can't choose to have a gun—you can only choose for the *other* person to have a gun. You can't make the other person start to cry to end the fight, but *you* can cry and end the fight. When I teach a variation in which someone cries to end a fight, I'll say that the person who cries is declared the winner of the game. No one ever takes that seriously but it's an idea I like.

It helps if people understand that they are not their character. In theater improv, people often make the mistake of trying to protect their character—keeping their character out of trouble, making their character win the fight—but you have to remember that *you are not your character*. You are the *author* of your character.

Sometimes in improv actors find themselves actually competing—fighting against each other to "win" a scene. These variations are a good way to train them out of that by jumbling up the definitions of what constitutes victory and what constitutes defeat.

I think these games teach you that victory and defeat within a scene don't constitute your own victory and defeat; that you as an actor can win the game by having you as a character lose the fight.

Sometimes people are too polite to each other in a scene because no one wants their character to be mean to the other character. Having people dance around doing victory dances while the other person weeps onstage, especially when it's the weeper who instigated this relationship, is a good way to train people out of that discomfort.

.

I started doing the argument games as music instruction because I suspected it would be a good way of loosening people up. I was working with a group of people and I wanted them to be making all sorts of interesting, crazy sounds. I wanted them to be using their bodies in interesting ways, and they were having a hard time with all of it. I thought that by having them fight, it might loosen them up a bit. And it did.

When people improvise musically, you want them to be able to really listen and respond to each other while making sounds at the same time. You want people to understand that it's sometimes okay to be quiet. You want people to have different ways of responding to their partner: sometimes joining them in what they're doing, sometimes repeating them, sometimes doing something completely different from what they're doing. And you want people to feel free to take the piece in a completely different direction.

It's really hard to teach people to do this straightforwardly with music, but it turns out that teaching people to do this with arguments takes about twenty minutes. So what I do is I teach people to argue, and then I tell them that a duet is just an argument except without anger, and the sounds you use don't have to sound like language anymore—they can be anything.

And very quickly people start to make interesting sounds and especially to make brave choices together, without the caution that usually typifies these things. It makes me very happy. There's a very pleasant paradox. It turns out that the best way to get people to communicate and collaborate on something beautiful is for them to start with a fight.

43. What Experimental Music Is For

It's a good thing to imagine that in experimental music and other art that uses the term *experimental*, you might want to take seriously the *experimental* tag. I think of it as the pure-research wing of a corporation or something like that. Most music aims to produce something of utility—in the sense that economists and philosophers use the word: something that people want, that brings them pleasure. People enjoy listening to this sort of music. They may even be willing to pay money to enjoy it. Experimental stuff, I feel, has a different goal, and it's just to produce lots of results and lots of new ideas, some of which might lead toward new ways of making that more obviously useful music.

Like, if you listen to "Work It" by Missy Elliott—that's pure pop: awesome, awesome, amazing, pure pop. It's exactly the opposite of the sort of research-and-development branch of the organization that is music. It's of tremendous immediate value. It makes people get up and dance. And people demonstrate the degree to which they value it by paying money to hear it, in different ways.

"Work It" is like this insane collage of incredibly abstract electronic noises, some of which would be considered really abrasive in other contexts. At various different moments, the vocal track is played backwards. But a song like "Work It" or any of a gazillion really interesting things happening now in dance music couldn't have happened without twentieth-century experimental music. It's as though "Work It" is the useful application of all those useless experiments. "Work It" is like those unbreakable dinner plates that got developed because of the space program.

44. These Projects Don't Make Money

It's really obvious to some people and not at all obvious to other people that the projects I run don't make any money at all. When people with real jobs read something about an art exhibition in a newspaper, or see a band interviewed on TV or featured on the cover of a local weekly, it's natural for them to assume that those people are making money. I mean, they're doing something that seems really successful. They're in the paper—you're not. So surely they must be making money.

For the past several years I've hosted the Trampoline Hall lecture series. When Trampoline Hall was doing really well, a friend of Sheila and her then husband, Carl, came up to them soon after they bought a house and said, *Wow, I guess the shows must be doing really well for you to be able to afford this house.* At the time, the show really was something of a little phenomenon. But it was a little phenomenon that happened once a month before a crowd of eighty people and charged five dollars at the door. And he wasn't joking! It's hard for people sometimes to understand that things that look successful or generate attention don't necessarily also generate money.

I feel it would be useful if the audience had a clearer understanding of what the economics really are. I always wanted to do a Trampoline Hall show about money, where part of the show would be to break down the budget of Trampoline Hall and explain to the audience how it came to be, and that we basically lost money doing this nominally successful show.

It's very hard to talk about this stuff. People want to appear successful, so they don't want to talk about how difficult it is to hold down a day job while working on their third album, but it's a big part of the reality of a lot of kinds of cultural production.

I'm not complaining. I'm not saying that there's an injustice here, or that artists need to be paid by society. I just think it's interesting that artists assume that the people in the audience have some sense of what the economics of their situation are, but in many cases they don't. I guess it would be great if audiences knew this stuff—if they could have more of a sense of patronage about the art that they enjoy and start to think about supporting the cultural things they like.

For instance, now, if I see a band that I like, I'll buy their CD—not because I want their CD at all, but because I understand enough about the economics involved to know that those CD sales are what keeps the band active, and that by buying a CD you're sort of casting your vote and doing your bit to make that possible.

It's tricky, because consumers of indie culture are often, by nature, bargain hunters. They're people who shop at thrift stores, and often they don't have much money. Being a bargain hunter and being a patron are sort of incompatible.

But the truth is, liking a really good band that no one knows about is typically a really good deal: you get to see them in small venues for not a lot of money; they'll probably answer your fan mail; they'll talk to you after a show. Seeing a band that everyone likes isn't much of a bargain. You typically have to pay more money to see them, you receive less attention or affection from them. When you do see them, you have to share that experience with more people, so you effectively get less from them.

Of course it's better for the *band* to be more popular. A bargain for the fan is often a bad deal for the artist. One of the secrets of Trampoline Hall is that people perceive—albeit not really consciously—that they're getting tremendously good value for their entertainment dollar. So, for five dollars they get a ticket that's usually handmade and a program at the door. They get to see three lecturers—a show that's the outcome of huge amounts of work that's only seen once before an audience of about a hundred people. The curator shakes their hands when they come in. There's a good chance that the host will acknowledge them individually in the audience. So they get a lot. Usually what makes these indie projects work is that the people who make them have motivations other than money—of course.

When I started getting involved in this kind of work, after years of being a computer consultant, I was continually baffled by just how impossible it was to make any money from all the exciting ideas I had.

I'm not sure I have gotten over that. It still remains a tremendous puzzle. The answer for me has been to take on a bunch of different projects that play off my interest in getting groups of people to do things together, and in the meantime try to arrange things so that some of what I do pays a lot of money—conferences and events like that. That way, I can offset the projects that pay very little money or lose money altogether.

Maybe that's okay. It means you have to try to think clearly about the benefits of each particular project; if there's not going to be money in it, what other benefits might there be? You have to be a bit more aware of why you're doing these things.

When I worked as a computer programmer, I wasn't—as computer programmers go—a particularly remarkable one: I didn't work very hard. I took lots of time off. I tried to only work three or four days a week. But I had tons of money, more money than I knew how to spend—which was great.

Slowly, as my life got taken over more and more by unprofitable art projects, and as more of my friends became people who were writers and artists, I tried to adapt a bit to my new circumstances, but I still find it hard. The way I live now is pretty extravagant by the standards of a performance artist, but very frugal by the standards of a computer programmer.

45. Seeing Your Parents Once a Week

Visit your parents once a week. Agree on the day, and see each other every week on that day. This is what I do. It helps because there are no negotiations about when I should see my parents, and there are no expectations or guilt on either side as a result of this agreement. I see them on Sunday nights, with my girlfriend. Usually they make or buy us dinner, and sometimes they even pick us up and drive us home, so it's okay.

46. Asking a Good Question

At Trampoline Hall, after every lecture, there's a Q&A with the audience. One of the things that's really great about the show is that the Q&A's really work. The audience asks really good questions. I think a big part of the reason they ask really good questions is that at every show, right at the beginning, I talk for a long time about what a good question is.

The first thing I tell people is that a good question has to be a question. I warn them that if they take a statement and try to raise the pitch of their voices at the end of their sentences, we won't be tricked. I tell the audience that grammarians will agree that there's no such thing as a two-part question. I tell people that if they think they have a two-part question, what they really have are two questions, and that they should just pick the better of the two.

I say that one way to tell if your question is any good is to look inside yourself. I ask the audience to pay attention to what feelings they have when they feel a question coming on. It may seem obvious, but curiosity is a good feeling to have. I say it's even okay if they feel a little bit angry and want to work that anger out by asking the lecturer something.

What I warn people against is feelings of pride. I ask them to pay attention to the pictures in their minds when they feel a question coming on, and if they see themselves becoming enormous and floating God-like above the audience, and the lecturer getting smaller and smaller in the distance, then maybe that's a sign the question isn't that great. I'm always careful to remind people that their bad questions are welcome; their good questions are just more welcome.

This speech—and I give it at the start of every Trampoline Hall show—is really long. It's sort of ridiculous and full of statements that people think are jokes. And they kind of are jokes, but the speech also really works. As much as anything, I think it really helps to let the audience know that they're expected to ask good questions.

So our events are not like other events where people go on forever without asking a question, or ask questions that are really off-topic. At Trampoline Hall, Q&A's are an incredibly pleasurable, enjoyable part of the show.

47. A Mind Is Not a Terrible Thing to Measure

There was an editorial in *The New York Times* by the psychoanalyst Adam Phillips, who I really like as a writer and a thinker, most of the time. The thrust of the article was that there should be no place for measurement in psychology; that when psychology falls into the hands of "scientists," they somehow ignore everything that is special and unique and mysterious about human beings.

Although it's not fair to hold a writer responsible for the title of an article, it was called "A Mind Is a Terrible Thing to Measure." Yet that was actually the point of the piece. It was pretty hard-core. The idea was that there's no place in psychology for empirical study or quantified measurement—as though if you *are* empirically curious about psychology, it somehow means that you don't think people have souls.

Phillips talks about "scientists" and "science," seemingly invoking these passionless men in white coats with slide rules who are going to measure your head and give you a pill and make you be more normal in society. But science doesn't have to mean that. I mean, first of all, scientists can care very much about the complexity of people's minds while also believing that the human mind is a phenomenon in nature, subject to some rules and worthy of empirical study.

He talks about how the standard of absolute predictability is unrealistic—and of course it is! No one thinks that the mind is absolutely predictable. I mean, the *weather* isn't predictable. Does that mean that meteorology isn't subject to scientific study?

Mostly what was frustrating, though, was this: I think what's ultimately meant by science—or *should* be meant by science—is a genuine curiosity about what's true and isn't true, empirically, in the world. So, for instance, it might be true that a good way to get over phobias is by talking a lot about one's early childhood experience of those fears. Equally, that might *not* be the case and it might not work. Gradual exposure to the thing you're afraid of might be a much more effective therapy. A really good way to find that out is by *looking at the world*, by looking at what happens when people are treated in these different ways, and seeing who actually gets over their phobias. That kind of looking is called science! That's what that is. That's *all*. And that's *so* important—to look at the world—to be willing to have your preconceptions or assumptions proven wrong by what the world has to say back to you when you test your assumptions out.

I think there's a real intellectual mistake at work here. *Of course* the human mind is tremendously complicated, and of course there's something very valuable in an attempt to construct meaning in one's life and out of one's experiences, and of course science can't do those things. But in many cases people go to psychotherapy to fix their problems, and it seems crazy and frankly wildly irresponsible to offer to help people with their problems while willfully and intentionally taking the position that empirical investigation into what solutions work is something you're emphatically uninterested in.

Empirically it might well be the case that results-oriented cures for specific psychological problems don't make things better, that the only answer lies in something more oblique and less solutions-oriented. That might be true. But even *that's* an empirical question.

To Adam Phillips, this may seem very rote and very "scientific" and mechanistic. It may seem like it's not terribly interesting—which maybe it's not. It may seem like it ignores a treasure trove of meaning which lies underneath our fears, which maybe it *does*. But if someone's life is being held back because air travel is impossible for them, they may want a solution to their problem. That seems fair.

In the article, he makes a big deal about how each session, each therapy, is unpredictable. Of course any treatment will work in some cases and not in others. But that is also true of all kinds of scientific phenomena, of all kinds of things. If, as a way to help people get over panic attacks, teaching breathing and relaxation exercises works 80 percent of the time, whereas talking about your childhood works 20 percent of the time, those are important facts to know.

Finally, Adam Phillips makes this comparison between psychotherapy and art. His belief is that science has real goals, whereas what art does is sort of shake things up, and it might make things better, and it might make things worse. It can't really make any promises. He thinks psychotherapy is like that.

Now, I agree with that about art, and I think there's a place in the world for things that shake things up in that kind of way, and that have uncertain outcomes. I think art *should* be like that. Psychotherapy probably shouldn't.

I can see why someone might want to go to a psychotherapist whose intention is to shake things up with uncertain outcomes—and have the therapy sessions be in that way like an art experience—but if you are the person offering that psychotherapy, I feel it's dishonest to not tell people, *Well, there's a guy down the block who says he can actually fix your problems.* And it's willful blindness to deny the possibility that that guy down the block might actually be able to do so.

Much of what Adam Phillips believes is that you have to accept uncertainty, that you can't know everything, which is something I tend to agree with. But you don't have to accept more uncertainty than you have to. The fact that you can't know everything doesn't mean that you shouldn't try to know anything.

48. Doing One Thing Doesn't Mean You're Against Something Else

When we do Trampoline Hall, we put amateur speakers onstage. People sometimes ask us why we are opposed to experts, but we are *not* opposed to experts. There's this terrible idea that the things you do are like this manifesto against everything else.

For instance, a few years ago, I was attending a conference about improvised music—specifically the difficult, experimental kind. One session at this conference was about whether it was okay to have melody and harmony and rhythm in improvised music. The people on the panel wanted to argue that it *was*. They perceived that there was a taboo against this, and they wanted to say that a truly improvised music—a music that was truly free—would allow for these things, because it should allow for anything. The whole question just seemed to me to be completely crazy. Music is not in the imperative mode. A piece of music isn't a universal command that dictates that all music should be like itself.

Usually in my noise classes I prohibit rhythm and melody and harmony, and I do that because in that particular exercise I specifically want to investigate what's possible without those things. Of course that doesn't mean I'm universally against those things—it just happens to be that I'm investigating something specific. I have to be strict because if I'm not, the investigation collapses. The purposes are local.

Like, if you write a book that takes place in Paris, it's not a statement that no book should ever take place in New York.

49. Get Louder or Quit

Lots of improvisations tend to end with a slow fading out, which I find really boring. I'm very interested in finding other types of simple endings. One instruction I really like for ending a piece is, *Get louder or quit*. This works especially well in a large group and the instruction is this:

Every few seconds, every member of the ensemble should check in on themselves and see how they're doing, and they can decide to do one of two things. They can drop out of the piece—and if everyone's standing, they can actually lie down and listen—or they can continue, but if they want to continue, they're obliged to become louder. Partly I like it because I like how it sounds—the gradual transformation from fifty people making soft sounds to ten people making louder sounds to two people screaming at the top of their lungs. But I also like that it discourages lazy group behavior. It says that it's okay and even interesting to stand out and go your own way in a piece. As an improviser, when you notice that most other people are becoming silent and dropping out of the piece, the joining inclination tells you that you should do the same thing—you don't want to be left behind; you don't want to be the gazelle that strays from the herd and gets killed by a lion. But being a good improviser is also very much about fighting that inclination. It's nice that while everybody else is quietly ending the piece, some people start yelling louder.

50. Why Robert McKee Is Wrong About *Casablanca*

One day, some friends and I snuck in to see the tail end of Robert McKee's seminar. Robert McKee is the author of *Story*, a sort of bible for screenwriters, and thousands of people pay lots of money to take his class. We arrived as he was talking about *Casablanca*, which is the grand finale of the seminar.

McKee says that what's so beautiful about *Casablanca* is Rick's great love for the Ingrid Bergman character. At the end, Rick chooses not to be with her, and McKee talks about this as the greatest illustration of the depth of Rick's love for her: it is *so strong* that it will live forever in Rick's heart, despite the tremendous physical distance that has separated them for years, and despite the fact that he now may never see her again.

I think Robert McKee might be a very bad husband. This seems like the most destructively romantic understanding of love. The idea that love is something magical, almost supernatural, in your heart, that has nothing to do with the day-to-day encounters with a real person—that understanding of love has probably created more unhappiness and ruined more marriages than just about anything.

Love is what happens between people living their lives together, becoming close through contact and actual partnership, and it's what survives through difficulties and imperfections. An idealized, imagined, faraway person in your heart—that's not love. That's a daydream. People often mistake that daydream for love, so either they're disappointed when love doesn't measure up to that daydream, or they try to protect that daydream from being sullied by real life.

A man like Rick—a man who chooses to be alone for his whole life out of love for a woman he chooses not to be with—isn't a man who knows anything about love.

51. Conferences Should Be an Exhilarating Experience

A big part of the work that I do is running a certain kind of conference that is usually called an "unconference." It's a name I don't like very much, but I think the structure is great. What defines these events is that they're super-highly participatory and they give the people attending them a tremendous amount of agency and control over what happens. If you're at one of these conferences, most of the time what's happening is you're engaged in conversation with people, and typically those conversations are conversations about the things you care most about, with the other people at the conference who also care most about those things.

I think that many conferences are organized without much thought given to why it is that people might come to a conference, or at least that's how they seem if you look at their design. So, for example, it seems to me that the main reason people would want to come to a conference has to do with actually meeting other people who share their interests, so that they can learn from each other or work together on solving problems. But what usually happens at a conference is you go into a room and you're in a room with fifty people and there's one person reading from their paper.

This structure is insanely atavistic! If you want to read this person's paper, you can read it on the Internet. This structure doesn't just ignore the existence of the Internet, it ignores the existence of the *printing press*. It's a medieval idea about how information should be disseminated—to imagine that if you want to know what someone thinks, you have to go sit in a room with them while they read out loud to you their thoughts. But at a lot of conferences that's the primary thing that happens.

Finding out what someone has to say in their paper isn't a reason to travel across the country and stay in a hotel room. A reason to travel across the country is to have conversations with people and actually form human relationships. Most of the stuff that happens at a conference not only does not help create that, it hinders it. You have all these smart people—say, ninety-nine smart, passionate people—sitting in silence as one person talks. And of those ninety-nine people, eighty of them are bored out of their heads. I think it's a huge waste of potential, all that intelligence and passion and interest just being switched off. Of *course* there are times when it's fun to hear a lecture, and that can be useful, but it really shouldn't be the only thing that a conference is about.

There's something called an "open space meeting" and there's something called an "unconference." An open space meeting is a super-simple, deeply self-organized structure, and an unconference is an event that typically includes an open space meeting alongside other structures.

Here's how an open space meeting works: You have a group of people and you let them write their own agenda. So maybe you'll have a hundred people coming together for a day and you have five time slots and six rooms for people to meet in. So you make a big, five-by-six-foot grid and you stick it up on the wall, and you say to this group of one hundred people, *Okay, who has something they want to talk about or learn about or work on?*

People say what they want to talk about, and you put it on the grid. This doesn't take very long, and now you've got this agenda where you're guaranteed that for every item on it, there's at least one person there who really cares about it. One thing I'll say to people is, *If there's something you really feel needs to be discussed today—if it's not up there, it's because you haven't put it there. It's not because of the failure of some conference committee; it's your job to put it there.* So you really try to ensure that all the things that people want to talk about are up there. You assign each topic a time slot and a room. Then you let people self-select and go into the rooms where the topics they most care about are being discussed. In any given room, there are any number of people who have chosen that one topic as being the thing they're most interested in talking about right then. If you've decided on that topic and you're in that room alone, you can think about that topic alone or go join another room. What turns out to be true is that a conference full of smart, passionate delegates can do a lot more and make better choices than a small conference-planning committee can.

Something else I say to people is that if you propose a topic at an open space meeting and only one person comes to your session, you might think that it's a failure, but to my mind it's this huge success: there's this one other person at the conference who cares about the thing you most care about, and you guys have *found* each other.

By doing all this, you eliminate a bunch of problems. You typically end up with pretty small groups, so almost everybody spends some time talking. You don't spend months with a conference committee trying to anticipate the desires of a group of people whose needs you ultimately can't anticipate. It generally works really well, and it also works well with different kinds of groups.

I did this kind of conference with workers in a very hierarchical health care organization that was experiencing cutbacks. The organization was going through changes that everyone knew were bad for everyone who worked there, and everyone felt discouraged. The goal was to look for ways to make it a better place to work in the face of all these cutbacks. The people at the conference weren't the managers; they were the frontline workers who took all the crap day-to-day, and who typically felt like they didn't have a lot of control. These were people who were thought of as incapable of a lot of organizational initiative. A lot of people thought, *Well, it won't work with this group. They're not initiative-takers. They're used to being told what to do*. But it worked so well. I've heard so many times, *It won't work with this group*, but it always works. It works well with groups of people who are really smart and really passionate and self-motivated, and maybe a little more surprisingly, it works amazingly with groups of people who are considered—or who consider themselves to be—the opposite of all those things.

When I'm designing an unconference, I'll spend a long time with the organizers figuring out how to seed conversations in ways that are useful. A really simple thing I'll do at the beginning of a conference is get people to put themselves into random groups. We used to program the groups, but it turns out it's better just to tell people, *Stand up and find four people you don't know*. Even that one step, something as simple as that—letting people form their groups very early on—really energizes the room differently.

Then what we'll do is give them specific topics of conversation. So we did a conference on copyright and art to which we invited artists and open-source software activists and legal experts and academics, most of whom were really opinionated. They were very engaged with the regulatory stuff that's going on in government, and I think if left to their own devices, the most natural starting point would have been for them to talk about the legal debates at that moment.

But as a starting point, once they were in random groups, we asked people to describe to each other early experiences that they could remember from their own adolescence, when there was a cultural product that they really, really coveted—a record they really wanted to hear or a book they wanted to read or a show they wanted to see—and we had them share those stories with each other, and it helped a lot, I think. It made people recall why this stuff is important to them. And also, you have someone sitting across the table from you and they hold some opposite position from you about the new bill being debated; eventually you'll find that out about them. But the starting point I'm more interested in is to hear them talk about that record that they were dying to listen to when they were fourteen years old, and how much that mattered to them, and to understand that everyone is at the conference because they care passionately about art, about culture, and to hear about those formative experiences—to gain the kind of personal intimacy that comes from hearing about those experiences.

After giving them a question like that, you reshuffle the groups and give them another question, and then you do it again. It takes just about an hour to do three conversations, and you've accomplished a huge amount. Every single person at the conference has met a dozen new people, so hundreds of connections have been made. Everybody at the conference has talked—which is unusual for a conference. And if it works well, people will really feel like they know each other, which I think is incredibly important.

A big problem that happens here in Canada, as in many places, is that we encourage people to immigrate who have professional training in their countries of origin, but when they come here, we don't let them practice their professions because we don't recognize their homeland's training. So we had an idea that a great conference would be one where we get all these people with foreign Ph.D.s who are driving taxicabs, and medical doctors who are working as security guards, and architects who are working as building superintendents—we'd get all those smart people together and have them spend a day thinking about some of the issues of immigration policy in Canada and write up a report.

We started the conference by asking people to go stand with people who came from the same continent as them. When you do this sort of exercise, you give people really minimal instruction and let them sort it all out themselves. It looked like a stock exchange floor with everybody shouting and waving and signaling at each other—figuring out who goes where. Southeast Asia split off from the rest of Asia; the Caribbean had its own group. Then we had people self-organize by professional training. The room sort of exploded into chaos at that point, and I had to reschedule everything I thought we were going to do, because for a lot of people, this was the first time in ten years that they'd been able to stand with a group of architects and identify as an architect, or stand with a group of doctors and be identified as a doctor. So you have a hundred people, all of whom are releasing years of pent-up frustration. It was really moving. I think we thought those two exercises would take only fifteen minutes, but they took an hour because people had so much to say to each other.

For the discussion part of the conference, I usually don't give too much instruction, but I have one tip that I'll give people. It's my "one over n" rule of conversation. What I tell people is: *If you're in a group of five people, the natural amount of time for you to be talking is about a fifth of the time.*

Whenever you tell people this, they laugh. Because the fact is so obvious, and the problems that arise from the nonrecognition of that fact are obvious, too. I'll tell people, *There's lots of good reasons to be talking more than that, and lots of good reasons to be talking less than that*, and I just kind of advise them: *If you are talking much more than that or much less than that, at the very least just stop and ask yourself if you have a good reason.* It doesn't work perfectly: dominant people still dominate sometimes and shy people are often more quiet. But I think giving the groups an awareness of this goal helps a lot.

I think what regularly happens at a conference is that the organizers will spend a lot of time thinking about who the panelists will be, and a lot of time thinking about what will be served for dinner. Lots of time is put into thinking of a theme for that year's conference, and if there's any thought at all put into the idea that people should talk to each other, they usually program a cocktail party. But a cocktail party is a *terrible* way for people to meet each other. If you're really outgoing, *maybe* you'll talk to ten new people, but you're not going to find the people at the conference you most need to talk to.

I went to one conference that was made up entirely of lectures and panels, and you had to fend for yourself to find lunch off campus, so when lunch came, which is the time you can talk to people, you weren't even all in the same place! Then they programmed a cocktail party, but they did the cocktail party as a fund-raiser, and they charged an extra fifty bucks on top of the conference admission fee to attend the fund-raiser. So there was one thing in the whole conference that was *actually* about getting people to meet each other, and they put a barrier in front of it!

I think that's really common, that kind of thinking. People figure that the social stuff will just work itself out.

52. Improvised Behavior

I like running improv theater classes but I don't really like the theater part very much. I like the running-around-behaving-foolishly part, but I'm not really interested in character or stories. In music, some people do work that doesn't involve melody or rhythm or pitch or any of the stuff that's traditionally characteristic of music. Eventually, with that really abstract stuff, you stop calling it "music" and just call it "sound." Similarly, in dance—when it starts becoming really undancelike, you just call it "movement." So I'm doing something that's like theater but dumber—classes without all the stuff that makes theater theater. I call these classes "improvised behavior."

53. Storytelling Is Not the Same Thing as Conversation

Mostly, I'm always suspicious when someone says, *Oh, that person's such a great conversationalist. They tell the most wonderful stories.* First off, being a conversationalist and telling wonderful stories aren't the same thing. I mean, a story isn't a conversation. It's a monologue, a one-way thing. When you're telling a story, you need to not be interrupted—and the story has to end up where you want it to end up.

The best conversationalists are people who are hoping to end up somewhere they didn't expect. I always picture storytellers at home, nervously rehearsing their anecdotes, so that when they get to the party, people will think well of them and be impressed. And that seems awful. It just seems sad to think of people sacrificing the potential pleasure of real conversation in the interest of scoring points.

It seems to me that the most pleasing thing you can find yourself saying in a conversation is something you haven't said before.

54. Introducing People in the Classes

When a new class begins, instructors often have a strong inclination to get people to go around a circle and introduce themselves, and maybe say why they're taking that class or what they hope to get out of it. I mostly try to resist this inclination.

People will get to know each other eventually. And there's something really nice about the time when people are starting to do these games together and the only thing they know about each other is, *That's the person with the red hair who likes to make deep, guttural noises.* It's like an innocence, almost, and like any innocence, it's sort of fragile and fleeting. I don't see what's really gained by knowing on the first day that a person works at a web design company or what their name is. It's kind of exciting for a little while not to have that information.

These classes are a really interesting way to get to know people. You see stuff about them that's so intimate, and you're doing something very unusual together, so there's a real bond. This bond isn't about having the kind of information that adults usually have about each other. It's about a shared experience. And you do get information about people, but just not the usual kind. You learn about how they use their bodies and how they use their voices, the times when they're bossy and the times when they're not. You get so much of that sort of thing so fast.

Something that's happened more than once in my classes is that at a certain point, maybe midway through a series, we'll be talking about some exercise or whatever, and one of the students will be talking, and I'll think, *Why are they talking in that weird voice?* Then I'll realize they're talking in their normal voice—it's just that I haven't heard it before. This is a person I've spent a few weeks watching and working with and thinking about, who I feel I know really well. But it turns out I don't actually know what their voice sounds like because I've never heard them speak.

55. Making the City More Fun for You and Your Privileged Friends Isn't a Super-Noble Political Goal

There are a lot of people out there who advocate a specific kind of civic improvement. They're interested in a kind of transformation of public space, and there's a cluster of causes that go together: less corporate advertising; more cycling and walking and less car use; outdoor events and street parties and bringing art to public places. There's a lot about this kind of work that's genuinely laudable, but what the city will end up looking like if such people achieve their goals is one that's uniquely and *specifically* well suited to people who are young and well educated and able-bodied, with a fair amount of free time, who are interested in culture and parties and living in a dense downtown core. In other words, people just like themselves.

Now, I mean, these goals, they're pretty well aligned with what *I* would like to see in a city. And they also happen to be preferences for things that are broadly pretty good. For instance, it probably *is* a good thing for people to be less reliant on cars. At the same time, it's easy to be opposed to cars when you and all your friends share a lifestyle built around walking and biking— for reasons that aren't actually environmental in origin.

I don't think it's terrible for people to push for their own self-interests in the design of a city, or to push for the interests and preferences of the groups to which they belong, but it's useful to have some recognition that this is what you're doing. The "more beautiful" city these people are picturing—with lots of posters for bands and garage sales stapled everywhere, which is permissive of graffiti, with street performers on every corner— this might be more beautiful to *them*. But I think, for instance, of my grandmother, a strongly opinionated woman who was born in a shtetl and had a fifth-grade education and whose husband worked in a garment factory. I think she would have *hated* to live in a city like that. Her image of beauty in a city would involve a lot more order and control and quiet, and it wouldn't be negatively impacted by some billboards depicting attractive models enjoying luxury products.

What I want is a lot closer to what these particular sorts of activists want than what my grandmother wants. But it's not fair, in the context of city planning, to pretend that the word *beauty* applies only to *my* image of beauty and not somebody else's.

You need to be smart to avoid the pitfalls of this sort of activism. I know some people who *are* pretty smart about it, but if you're not careful, you end up being part of this long and unadmirable tradition of educated, cultured people who want to promote everything that's good and uplifting, and cleanse the city of everything that's bad for it. And it just happens that the things that are good for the city are the things that members of the educated, cultured class happen to enjoy, and the things that are bad for it are the things they don't.

There's something in this mentality that feels like it's about trying to protect the city from itself—trying to protect it from commerce. All this agitation against advertising in public places in the city—I mean, a city is an *inherently* commercial place. What creates a city is people coming together to do trade with each other. It's *fundamentally* a place of commerce. So to object that advertising is impinging on our public space is really to take an imaginary and high-minded understanding of what a city is and what a city is for.

56. Seeing John Zorn Play Cobra

I saw John Zorn play Cobra when I was a student. It must have been when he was first starting to perform it. There are these people onstage juxtaposing all these discordant noises and snippets of music, and they're all making hand signals at each other and waving cards with cryptic symbols on them. Then someone puts on a hat and someone takes off a hat. It was all pretty crazy and baffling to watch.

They did the performance, and then at the end of the performance they had time for questions. So I asked what seemed to be the only reasonable question to ask, which is, *How does this game work?* John Zorn seemed pretty emphatically to think that was a dumb question. He said something like, *I don't want to explain how this game works. I don't think that's the point. This is a piece of music, and if I had my way, we'd be playing it behind a screen and the audience would just be listening to it.*

I think I said, *Well, I think it would be more fun for the audience and more interesting if we knew what was going on.* He didn't take well to that.

Naturally, if he really wanted to play the game behind a screen, he *could*. People have played the game all over the world for twenty-five years, and, to the best of my knowledge, no one has ever played it behind a screen. So the performance of this game, by *design*, always involves a bunch of people onstage doing something very complicated and very intriguing that's completely incomprehensible to the audience, then curiously making the statement that the audience shouldn't be intrigued.

A long time later, I was running a games night. The idea was that I'd get people into a bar and have them play different games together—they would play Jenga or charades. Then I got the idea to play Cobra. I was still really interested in undoing that crazy obfuscation that was in the John Zorn performance. There was something in it that seemed wrong to me—the idea of a bunch of performers onstage sharing this inaccessible inside joke among themselves, which the audience is somehow challenged to not care about or something.

The rules of Cobra are secret to some degree. John Zorn has always insisted that they not be published anywhere, so they're passed on orally from musician to musician, all of whom promise to keep that code of confidentiality. At the time, there was a bit of a Cobra scene in Toronto, run by a musician named Joe Sorbara, and when I approached Joe about wanting to run a game of open Cobra, he was initially reluctant. But eventually I think he figured that my Cobra would be sufficiently helpful to the cause of improvised music and didn't constitute too much of a violation of John Zorn's requirements, since we wouldn't actually be publishing the rules.

The show worked like this: First Joe's band came on and played Cobra the way it's normally played, in all its noisy, inaccessible mystery. I had written a really simple computer program which was called the Cobratron, which was something between a scoreboard and a series of educational flash cards that we projected above the stage, so the band could play demonstration rounds of Cobra, while the Cobratron gave a live play-by-play of what was happening, explaining the game. Then we took a short intermission and I said to people, *Come back and we'll make some sounds together for a few minutes, and if you like that, you can stick around and learn Cobra.* I also said, *If you don't like it, which is a really, really normal response, then you can leave, and that's okay.*

After the break, about three-quarters of the people returned, and I had them do some noise exercises. Then a few more people left, but the vast majority stayed. It was exciting, since this was a self-selected group of people who all knew that this was something they liked. It was also a room of people who had only discovered two minutes ago that this was something they liked.

Cobra is an insanely complicated game, and I wanted to create as much proficiency as quickly as possible. A lot of the training was done in small groups—so we had a whole barroom of people gathered in small clusters, simultaneously booing and hissing and barking. It was real chaos, real cacophony, but by the end of the evening, they were playing Cobra, and they were thrilled to be watching each other, and sort of applauding wildly.

While the game had at first seemed completely opaque and inaccessible and like uninteresting noise, people started to find beauty in these previously cacophonous sounds, and they began developing aesthetic preferences, and they started to find that some sets of cacophonous sounds were more beautiful to them than others. As I'd guessed twenty years ago, the game was a lot more interesting to the audience once they had some insight into what was going on.

57. Impostor Syndrome

There's this phenomenon called "impostor syndrome," and it describes situations in which accomplished people who have admirable jobs or high positions feel like they're impostors—that they're fakes—and worry that someone will discover that they're not really qualified to do this thing. I think it's natural for people to feel this way, and smart, accomplished people often do feel insecure. But it often gets talked about as a sort of psychological problem that people have.

One possibility I think people often overlook is that there might be people who feel this way because they *are* impostors. There actually *are* people who hold impressive jobs or high positions who don't merit them.

It's normal for us to feel insecure about our own real abilities or accomplishments, but it's also the case that we're kind of encouraged to lie about our abilities and successes. There is so much pressure on people to achieve, to become ever more accomplished and impressive, and that goes along with this encouragement to be a kind of salesman of yourself in a certain way. So what ends up happening is that a lot of people really *are* presenting a version of themselves that is false. In this case, the reason they have this unpleasant feeling of being an impostor is because they are one.

The solution to impostor syndrome may not be in getting people to accept that they really are who they say they are, but rather to stop pressuring people into lying so much.

58. Nimbyism

Our Residents' Association continues to try to control the number of new bars in our neighborhood, and so we get called Nimbys a lot—which, for those who don't know, is a disparaging term that stands for Not In My Back Yard. It refers to neighborhood groups who stop things from happening.

It always seems strange to me that the word is derogatory, because it's great and important for people to be concerned about what happens in their neighborhood. It's not as if a general problem in our society is that we suffer from an excess of civic engagement. In Toronto, for instance, interesting neighborhoods get overrun with bar monocultures precisely because residents don't feel a kind of neighborhood pride or ownership, or don't have strong enough communities to be able to really take charge in the places they live. And I think that's a real problem.

So it doesn't seem at all bad for people to stand up and say, Not In My Back Yard—for people to want to take charge of what happens around them. It does seem bad to have laws and institutions in place that let the evolution of a neighborhood be determined entirely by the interests of businesses and not at all by the interests of people who actually live there.

At the same time, I'm aware, even in my own case, of the dangers of this kind of activism. You don't want a city, for instance, that has no nightlife in it at all, even though someone who lives beside a newly opened bar might prefer that it didn't exist. And of course, the much more serious issues about which the Nimby term typically gets used—like for people who don't want a homeless shelter nearby, or a halfway house, or people different from themselves—make it clear that it's important to limit the amount of say that people have in what happens in their neighborhoods, too.

The best results happen from balancing different people's desires. You can't villainize people for wanting to have some say in what happens in their own neighborhood, but neither can you expect that everything that happens in your neighborhood is up to you to decide.

59. Conducting from the Center of a Circle

You get the whole group into a circle. Then you put one person in the center of the circle. The idea is that they close their eyes, which in most of these games sort of indicates that they're the audience, and they conduct the whole ensemble by moving around. So they're both the audience and the conductor at the same time, which is a combination I really like. Because their eyes are closed, they're in less of an authoritative role than the conductor is in some of the other games. I encourage them to lose themselves in it a bit. I'll often spin them around a little bit and rearrange the members of the ensemble to discourage the person from having too much of a sense of what's going on. The person in the middle can do whatever they want to evoke or alter sounds from the ensemble. I encourage them to think about timbre, about how they can affect the *kinds* of sounds that people make. People tend to use their bodies in really interesting ways in this exercise. Because they're in the center of a circle and because they can't see what they're doing, the connection between gestures and sounds is a little bit looser in some ways. Also, because they're listening with their eyes closed as they're doing this, they're responding to the sounds as they do this—which is to say, dancing. It seems to me that that's sort of the difference; conducting is when you make movements to alter a sound, and dancing is when you make movements in response to a sound. Part of what's nice about this game is that you're doing a bit of both simultaneously. It's a pretty wonderful experience, I think, for the people playing it.

It's especially exciting if the conductor can forget, even a little bit, what's going on—can forget that people they know are responding to their gestures—and lose themselves in the more abstract experience of a soundscape responding to their movements.

60. Why Noise Music?

A hundred and fifty years ago, if you wanted to hear music in the house, you taught your daughter to play the piano. It made sense to teach your daughter to play the piano, because it was the only way you could hear piano music on a regular basis. It really solved a practical problem. But now learning to play an instrument is like churning your own butter or something. It's not actually a necessary or efficient way of getting music into your world.

The music made by people in my classes ends up being atonal, experimental noise music, not so much because I'm so interested in atonal, experimental noise music, but because I want to give people a chance to enjoy making sounds together. Yet I don't want it to feel like I'm teaching people to churn their own butter. I feel like if you learn to play "good" music on an instrument, you can't escape the amateurism trap, where you're imitating the professionals, and playing the sort of stuff you hear on the radio, but worse. But most people have no preconception of what noise music is supposed to sound like, so when you just make noise music, you're released from that kind of baggage. You're not trying to imitate a professional out there doing the "real" thing better than you.

61. Absenteeism

I think that for a lot of people my class is the most fun they will have all week, if not all year. But the experience of *anticipating* one of these classes somehow isn't fun. I think what most people feel immediately before the class is trepidation. I think that's true even for the sixth class of an eight-week series, and you'd think they would have learned or gotten used to it. But there's no getting around it. It's scary. It's like getting into the lake when you go swimming. There's that first moment of getting into the water, and it's unpleasant. Then you're swimming and it's great. But no amount of knowledge about that gets you past the feeling that you might not want to swim.

This creates a problem with absenteeism. People call and say they're feeling not quite right for the class today; work was really stressful, or they're a little under the weather and they're not quite in the right mood—and I always just tell them to come anyhow. If I can convince them to come to the class, they inevitably overcome their self-diagnosed state of not being in the right mood for it. They have a great time and the class takes them out of the class-inappropriate mood.

I think it's important to say that I go through those exact same feelings before I teach the classes. It's probably my favorite thing in the world to do, but before every single class I secretly hope that no one will show up and it will be canceled.

62. Failure and Games

If you're worried about failure, then it's very hard to let yourself be surprised. If you're thinking you shouldn't fail, then probably you imagine that there's somewhere in particular you need to be. You're probably intent on taking a particular path to get there. So if you find yourself somewhere surprising, you might feel the need to go backwards, to get back onto the right path. That means you'll miss out on a lot of interesting and useful surprises.

It's good to learn to suspend the fear of failure. Game structures can be very useful for that, because failure is built into games. If you're playing baseball and you swing at the ball and you don't hit the ball, you understand that's part of the game. It wouldn't be a very good game if you always hit the ball. What mostly happens is you swing at the ball and you *don't* hit. Does that mean that playing baseball is a miserable experience because you're mostly failing? If you miss the ball playing baseball, it doesn't mean you're playing baseball wrong. It just means you're playing baseball.

63. Why a Computer Only Lasts Three Years

People complain about how *in our modern world* things aren't built to last. So when you buy a phone, for instance, it breaks after two or three years and you have to buy another one, and the same with a computer, whereas it used to be that you could buy a typewriter or a telephone and it lasted for decades.

I see this as a pretty benign consequence of progress. The typewriter that lasted for fifty years wasn't built in a world where the machines we type on become a hundred times more powerful every three years. Would it really be so awesome if the DOS-based 8086 IBM PC that you bought in 1983 still functioned today? Presumably it would have cost twice as much to make that machine last that long. Now, for less than a week's salary for the average person, you can buy a machine that can access all the information in the world while copying a movie and storing more text than is contained in a floor of a university library. So you can buy this machine that does all these incredible things, knowing that in three years a machine will come along that does all those things and more, even more incredibly.

This built-in obsolescence doesn't come out of malevolence. It comes out of the breakneck speed of progress. We get so insanely much for our money. These machines are such incredibly great deals. And the return on the money accelerates so fast. There's no sense in the manufacturer spending extra money to make this year's machine durable enough to compete with the machines that will be around in three years.

64. What Are These Classes For?

When I run events and teach classes, I generally pretty much avoid talking about what I imagine they might be for. With my music classes, for instance, I want to imagine that they can be very different things for different people. So I know why *I* like to do them, but a lot of those reasons aren't transferable to the people in my classes, because these reasons have to do with my experience of leading the class, not their experience of taking the class. People are sometimes interested in thinking about the classes as being for specific purposes—that the classes will help them be more confident or flexible in some situations, or that they'll learn something about music or theater, or that the classes will help them relax or be more creative.

It's really important to me that my classes aren't meant to bring about some specific result. I guess in some real way this means they're not actually classes, even though in many ways they resemble classes.

With my music classes, what I mostly want is for them to be a musical experience for people. I want them to have functions similar to music. If people ask what the classes are for, well, they're for whatever music is for. When a person makes a record, it might be the case that someone likes to put on that record after work to help them relax, but that doesn't mean that that's what the record is—an after-work relaxing machine.

One of the most flattering responses a student had to one of my early music classes—and flattering only maybe to me—was that he missed one week and came back the week after. I asked why he wasn't there, and he said he hadn't been feeling great that week. One thing that I happen to know about these classes is that a lot of the time if you come to the class when you don't feel like it, you find that you get really into it, and that it cheers you up and takes you out of that bad mood or whatever. I described that to him, and started explaining that to him, and he interrupted me and he said, *Yeah yeah yeah, I understood that if I came to the class it would probably fix my bad mood, but I didn't want to start thinking about the class as a sort of therapy that I used to raise my spirits.*

This is almost puritanical, I guess, but it really pleased me— the idea that he thought it would trivialize the class to think of it as a sort of therapy.

65. Who Are Your Friends?

Teaching my classes, I started to notice during the breaks that there was so much warmth between these people who often had very little in common. They had engaged in a fairly passionate and intimate kind of play with each other, and the connections between them happened so quickly, and they developed such a collective fondness for each other. But this fondness lacked the traits we normally associate with adult friendship. They didn't know that much about each other. They didn't know what was going on in each other's lives. But they felt a strong and genuine closeness. They were happy to see each other. And I started to think, *Oh—friends are the people you play with*. That seemed like a pretty good definition of friendship to me, and I was satisfied with it.

Then, about five years ago, a friend of mine moved here from Kelowna, British Columbia. She said, *You know, in Toronto, friendships are all based around talking. What you do with your friends is you go out for coffee or drinks, or you go to their apartment and you talk about stuff. In Kelowna, what you do with your friends is go swimming.* It seemed really beautiful to me that in Kelowna your friends might just be these people who liked floating around in the water with you—that the people floating near you are your friends.

66. Neighborhoods Change

Neighborhoods, inevitably, change. Sometimes they change in ways you don't like. You might be sad, for instance, to see the old Italian working-class neighborhood you live in get taken over by yuppies that work at ad agencies, but there's no law against that. No one should have the right to choose who their neighbors are. But people do have the right—to some limited degree—to say what kinds of businesses can operate in their neighborhood, and what kinds of buildings can be built.

I may be upset, for instance, that my neighborhood has become a place where lots of trendy souvenir shops are opening, but I don't think for a moment that I should have the right to stop trendy souvenir shops from opening, just because I happen to dislike them. I dislike having nightclubs nearby, too, but I think nightclubs are different: I think people *do* have the right to regulate nightclubs in their neighborhood. It's not like I think nightclubs aren't good or important. They are. They're something a city really needs to have. But a nightclub next to a home is in the business of selling off other people's peace and quiet. Not every kind of business is allowed everywhere. In most places, there are laws that prohibit you from operating, say, a slaughter-house or an iron-smelting plant on a residential street. I think a nightclub is like that. Having a nightclub next door makes an apartment effectively unusable.

It's really important to distinguish the things you might not like in a neighborhood from the things over which you *oughtn't* to have control. It's important to make these distinctions, because limits on our control are kind of fundamental to democracy. So a lot of people might not want to have a gay bookstore nearby, or a lot of people might be dismayed to find more members of ethnic minorities moving into their neighborhood, or, for that matter, rich hipsters. But in those cases, your neighborhood preferences lose against the general principles of freedom. As much as I may hate the cute gift store or annoyingly trendy dinner restaurant on my block, I recognize that it's important that I not have the right to oppose them.

67. Atheism and Ritual

A lot of the society around us is becoming more secular and less religious, and I think that's a great thing. I mean, mostly, I think it's really good that we not believe in superstitious falsehoods. But it seems to me that there's a good chance that there's something about people that makes us really *need* a lot of that stuff. So one answer is that we continue to believe in superstitious falsehoods because there's something about us that makes us need them, and another is that we sort of demand of ourselves to get over superstitious falsehoods and stop believing them.

I guess what I sort of want to imagine is that there might be some way to refuse to believe things that aren't true, while also respecting that part of what it means to be a human is to need some of the things that often go along with those beliefs. I guess I'm thinking of things like once-useful rituals that have become meaningless, or a sense of the sacred that we no longer experience, or something like that.

I think it's hard to figure out how to have those things in our lives without a sort of crazy false belief at the center of them, but I have a hope that it might be possible. Still, to move in that direction, you have to accept that humans aren't just these hyperrational thinking machines that have been making an analytic mistake all these centuries. You have to see us more as these beings who really do crave some sort of connection to something mysterious and bigger than ourselves, and you have to understand this craving as something real, and possibly important, that you can't just reason out of existence.

Some people do meditation without an attachment to any

particular religious tradition—that feels connected to what I'm thinking of. It feels funny to say it, but I think I have some of these issues in mind when I teach the music classes. People come to a space and they do something very different from their day-to-day life that has a component of ritual, that can make them feel like they're connected to something that's sort of magic, but without having to actually believe that the rules of science are being suspended.

Sometimes people in my classes *do* want to take more literally spiritual interpretations of what's going on—like that they're in touch with something genuinely magical in the universe. What's specifically interesting to me is the possibility of having that feeling of things being somehow magical, and respecting that feeling as something really important and interesting and exciting, without having to imagine there's anything going on that's literally magical in the sense of being supernatural.

It broadly excites me to think that people might get better at finding things like this in the secular world; that in the future people might be able to engage this side of themselves that wants to lose themselves in a way, but without having to abandon an attachment to the truth to do it.

68. Social Capital

A lot of people I know who work in the arts think they're poor. And it's true that some of them might not have much money, but the idea that they are somehow "the poor" is, I think, an idea too ridiculous to even merit serious consideration.

69. Sitting Down and Listening as a Role

In many of the games I do, one role a person can take is to be the person sitting with their eyes closed and listening. I don't do this in every game, but in some. At some level, it seems important to indicate that people listening are part of the process. I'm closing a kind of loop; the game remains a social thing among the people who are present, and is not a rehearsal for some imagined future audience. Many of the games that I do are kind of theatrical. They involve a lot of moving around and interacting, and that can be fun to watch. Making people periodically stop and just listen serves to remind them to think about the sound output, to understand that at some level all that running around and theater is a means to an end—the end of sound.

Here is a basic listening game:

If it's a class of ten people, I'll ask four people to volunteer to sit down with their eyes closed in different parts of the room. Then I'll ask another four to choose to be sound-makers. The remaining two people are spectators. It's a funny distinction—between listener and spectator—but it feels like an important one to me. The ones sitting on the floor with their eyes closed—even though they're not doing anything other than listening—I somehow want them to be understood to be part of the piece, while the two people sitting on the couch and listening are not.

Then I'll ask the four sound-makers to start making sounds. Often I'll start this game after we've been doing some argument games, so the sounds they make are abstract and argument-like. The four sound-makers start having sound dialogues with each other, and while they're engaged in that sort of theatrical activity, moving around the room, the listeners are primarily just having a sound experience. The piece, of course, sounds completely different to each listener, which is something I really like, and the sound-makers quickly understand the listeners as an element to be played with—whispering in people's ears or sneaking up on them and making loud noises.

Then you shuffle the roles and play again. People keep experiencing the game from different perspectives: sometimes watching it from the outside as a spectator, sometimes hearing it only as sound, sometimes participating in it. I think people get a greater insight into the game by being shuffled through those different roles.

70. Everyone's Favorite Thing and Unfavorite Thing Are Different

Over the course of an eight-week class we'll do maybe fifteen different games and exercises, and I'll sometimes check in with people halfway through or toward the end of the classes to see what people have liked, and it's always really surprising. There will be some particular person who I thought really hated some particular exercise, and then their complaint will be that we didn't play it long enough.

Usually what I find is that, if the class is any good, pretty much everything we do will be at least one person's favorite thing and one person's least favorite thing. I think this is really useful to understand as a teacher or an organizer of things like this. It's easy to get caught up in imagining that the whole group really loved something, or really didn't like something, and to worry about it, too.

It's both reassuring and frustrating to understand that, whatever you do, some people are going to like it and some people won't.

It can be useful for the students in the class to know this, too. If there's some exercise they're really disliking, they'll experience it differently if they understand that somebody else in the class is probably really enjoying it.

71. Finding an Ending

When I have people doing improvisations together, I'll often have some signal that means they should find an ending. I'll ring a bell or sometimes I'll throw something at them. At first, people will just stop playing when I do that. Then I'll say, *No, no, you can keep playing—you just have to end it.* Then what they'll do is keep playing, but maybe a little less. Eventually they get the idea of what it means to find an ending, and what happens pretty quickly is that people get better at it; people begin to take more responsibility for what's happening in the piece. They let things go in some sudden, brief new direction. They play as if the next bit really matters. They take additional risks, and are somehow freer than they were before. I wish I could find a way to get people to always be engaging with that intensity and that degree of intention. It turns out that telling people, *Find an ending*, is like saying, *Play a little bit better for a while, and then stop.*

72. Wearing a Suit All the Time
Is a Good Way to Quit Smoking

I used to smoke a lot. I smoked more than anybody, I think— like, two and a half packs of cigarettes a day, and in Canada, there are twenty-five cigarettes in a pack, so I was smoking over sixty cigarettes a day. I was *always* smoking.

Sometimes, I would be at a party and find myself reaching for a cigarette to light, only to realize I was already smoking one. And of course, smoking two cigarettes does not make you look twice as cool as smoking one.

So I smoked a lot. And also—because I'm someone who worries—I really took seriously the issue of being addicted to cigarettes. So, for instance, if I had to take a two-hour plane ride, I would stock up on Nicorettes. If I had to take a two-hour train ride, I had a special device which would allow me to smoke in the bathroom without detection.

I really liked smoking. But I also understood that it was bad for you.

I tried to quit smoking when I was in college. I understood smoking to be a physical addiction, so I thought the important thing was to overcome the physical addiction, which of course could only be done by not smoking.

I also figured—and here was my miscalculation—that you couldn't maintain a physical addiction if you had, say, just a couple of puffs of a cigarette each day.

So I stopped smoking, but once in a while I would have a couple of puffs off a friend's cigarette. Maybe at the end of the day I would have a haul or two off my roommate's cigarette. In effect what I was doing was making smoking the reward for quitting smoking. This is not a good mechanism, and it did not work or last very long. And though I think it's probably true that I overcame my physical addiction to nicotine, the physical addiction is just a small part of how these things work.

After that, I didn't consider trying to quit for a very long time. I just kept on smoking for fifteen years, pretty much nonstop, sometimes while swimming, sometimes in the middle of the night as a little break from sleeping. It was always kind of a bad time to quit, so I didn't.

I think the thing that really got me was taking a trip to Las Vegas. I really liked it there, but it also seemed so terrible to see the worst things about people all together—how easily people are controlled by money, and how easily people can be made to feel good about themselves when gambling because of something that happened by chance. Everything about the place sort of seemed like a study in how people's appetites and cravings mislead them.

And you can smoke *everywhere*.

So I smoked more in Vegas than I'd ever smoked, all the time kind of thinking about these people around me who seemed like they were being tricked by everything. They were being tricked by these gambling games, they were being tricked by the problem of having a certain kind of job that required that you take a certain kind of vacation which was organized around a certain set of hopes about money, but the trick that clearly was working on me better than just about anyone else was the cigarette trick.

I think it was there that I really decided that I needed to quit soon. *Soon* in this case meant three years later.

Up until then, I was always starting a new job or ending a job, or starting a relationship or ending a relationship, or any of a million other reasons for which it was an inconvenient time to quit, but in the spring of 2000 I ran out of excuses. I decided I'd approach quitting smoking with the same passion and enthusiasm as I had approached smoking.

So I read lots of books on the subject. I went to a 12-step-style smoking-cessation group. I found a psychotherapist who specialized in smoking-cessation programs. It was a months-long project. I did all kinds of things. I switched to a brand I didn't like—from du Maurier to Player's—ever switching to lighter and lighter cigarettes.

Mostly, the books say that cutting down isn't especially effective. So I did cut down, but what I really tried to do was train myself out of all the individual habits related to smoking. I was afraid that once I quit smoking, I wouldn't be able to work anymore, so, long before I quit, I made it a rule for myself that I couldn't smoke while I was working, so I could learn how to work without smoking. I was worried I wouldn't be able to not smoke while drinking, so, before I quit, I practiced drinking and not smoking. I practiced talking to girls at parties. That was a big one. I think a big breakthrough for me was when a girl left a party with me and I hadn't been smoking.

Through all of this, I didn't actually stop smoking. For instance, in the middle of my work, I would go outside and have a cigarette, then return to my smoke-free working. I think, in the same way, I probably excused myself while I was talking to that girl to go leave the party and have a cigarette.

Let me make it clear that I understand all of this is completely crazy.

I'll give you what really is useful advice for anyone who wants to quit and doesn't want to be or *isn't* necessarily crazy. The big secret for quitting smoking, compared with a lot of other things, is that it's pretty simple. To quit smoking, all you need to do is make the decision that you will never smoke again.

Now, this isn't true about losing weight and it isn't true about a million other decisions one might make in one's life that require nuance or are questions of degree or are complicated tasks. But with smoking it's really simple. If you make the decision never to inhale tobacco smoke again as long as you live, you'll be okay.

That means a few things. Mostly, it means you make no exceptions. You can't smoke once in a while. You can't, as I did, smoke as a reward for not smoking. You can't act as if it's a big surprise when things in your life get difficult. You have to decide that you will not start smoking when there are crises in your life. People say, *I'm going to quit*, but then there's some crisis—they get fired from their job, their relationship ends, there's a death in their family—and they start smoking again. But there are always crises. In my case, the crisis that triggered my starting again in university was the exam period—a crisis which you might think I could have seen coming.

If your strategy for quitting smoking is, *I'm not going to smoke again unless something bad happens in my life*, it's a pretty safe bet that in ten years you'll be smoking again. It's pretty easy to quit for a year, but the goal really is to not start again ever.

The one thing that the smoking-cessation therapist said to me that stuck with me was that terrible things happen in one's life. That's normal. So, she pointed out, for instance, that in a sort of best-case, normal, happy life, both one's parents will die. For most people this is a terrible, sad, stressful thing. And while day-to-day that occurrence is certainly out of the ordinary, in the scheme of a full life, it's about the most normal thing that can happen. She specifically said, *You have to think about your parents dying and not starting smoking again when that happens.* I thought that was nice.

I had my quit date planned out months in advance. Finally that day came, and I smoked my very last cigarette outside in my backyard, because that was the only part of my house that I allowed myself to smoke in anymore.

My friend Chris had promised to buy me lunch at Mr. Greenjeans at the Eaton Centre that day, so I was on my way to meet Chris, and I figured, *This is a special day. I think I'll wear a suit.*

So I put on a suit that I bought for a cousin's wedding and I went out to meet Chris.

To be honest, I always kind of liked wearing a suit, but there were few occasions when it was really appropriate for me. But I figured this was a special day, so what the hell. I went to Mr. Greenjeans with Chris, and it was okay, this not smoking. I felt a little dizzy, I had a little bit of a headache, but it wasn't too bad. It was nice to have that day with Chris.

The next day I woke up.

I put so much time into thinking about my first day quitting smoking, but I hadn't thought that much about my second day. So I figured, *Well, wearing that suit yesterday seemed to work out for me. Maybe I'll wear it again. I mean, it seems sort of inappropriate, but what the hell. I'm quitting smoking.*

The books often tell you that when you're quitting smoking, you should give yourself little rewards. My little reward was to let myself wear a suit. So I wore a suit on the second day, and again on the third day. For my first month quitting smoking, I pretty much wore a suit all the time, even at home. The same suit.

It was kind of great. I'd run into people on the street and they'd say, *Hey, why are you wearing that suit?* And I'd say, *I'm quitting smoking*—as if that explained it. But it was good having this quitting-smoking suit. Like it gave me powers or something.

I also bought a really expensive yo-yo, which I carried around with me for a while, until my twelve-year-old cousin told me to stop. I think he was right. The yo-yo went too far. We were walking around Kensington Market and I was in my suit, in which I should say I looked somewhat ridiculous with my then long, greasy hair. I didn't look like a normal guy in a suit. I looked like someone in a costume, walking through Kensington Market, doing yo-yo tricks. My cousin said, *Why don't you just get a monocle and start walking a tiny dog or something?* And I understood he had a point, so I started leaving the yo-yo at home.

I think what most made me nervous about the prospect of quitting smoking was that it was a project that was completely occupied by negative space. I mean, I know how to take on a project if it consists of doing something, but here this whole project consisted of *not* doing something. It's hard to know how much time to allot for a project that consists entirely of not doing something.

Now I'm sort of known for wearing suits. I'll always wear a suit if I'm performing, and I usually wear a suit if I'm going to a party or something like that, and I'll often be the only person wearing a suit. These aren't suit parties I go to. But it's funny, because you sort of grow into wearing a suit, which is nice. It makes getting older a little easier.

The suit is often described in the press as "wrinkled," and I'm frequently described as "a man in a wrinkled suit." I'm not sure why this is. I have the suit dry-cleaned and pressed pretty often, and it's rarely wrinkled. I'm not sure why people would think my freshly pressed suit is in fact wrinkled. It must just be something about me.

Acknowledgments

Thanks to Mitzi Angel, Chantal Clarke, Kathy Daneman, Susan and Sholom Glouberman, Dave Meslin, Darren O'Donnell, Lucas Rebick, Patrick Roscoe, Erik Rutherford, Leanne Shapton, Lorin Stein, Duane Wall, Margaux Williamson, Carl Wilson, and Jacob Wren.